BERLITZ®

GREA
MIAMI

1989/1990 Edition

By the staff of Berlitz Guides
A Macmillan Company

How to use our guide

- All the **practical information,** hints and tips that you will need before and during the trip start on page 108.

- For **general background,** see the sections The City and the People, p. 6, and A Brief History, p. 15.

- All the **sights** to see are listed between pages 28 and 79. Our own choice of sights most highly recommended is pinpointed by the Berlitz traveller symbol.

- **Sports, shopping, entertainment** and all other **leisure activities** are described between pages 79 and 93, while information on restaurants and cuisine is to be found on pages 94 to 103.

- Finally, there is an **index** at the back of the book, pp. 127–128.

Found an error in this Berlitz Guide? Or a change or new feature we should know about? Our editor would be happy to hear from you, and a postcard would do. Be sure to include your name and address, since in appreciation for the most useful suggestions, we'd like to send a free travel guide.

Although we make every effort to ensure the accuracy of all the information in this book, changes occur incessantly. We cannot therefore take responsibility for facts, prices, addresses and circumstances in general that are constantly subject to alteration.

Photography: Aram Gesar; pp. 7, 9, 14, 45, 51, 71, 82, 95, 98, 102 Jacques Bétant.
Layout: Doris Haldemann
We are particularly grateful to the staff of the Greater Miami Convention & Visitors Bureau for their help in the preparation of this book.
4 Cartography: 𝐹𝑎𝑙𝑘 Falk-Verlag, Hamburg.

Contents

Cover picture: Miami Beach from the air
Pages 2 and 3: On the oceanfront, Miami Beach

The City and the People

Miami's geographical and cultural position brings a unique flavour to the great American tradition of cosmopolitan life. Largest city of the southern United States, it has become in many ways the northernmost city of South America.

Up in the gleaming glass and steel skyscrapers of the banking and business districts, the city provides a vital link in financial relations between North and South America. Down in the streets, the smells and sounds of Miami

may recall the delicatessens and supper clubs of New York and New Jersey, strong Cuban coffee and cigars and perhaps the exotic beat of Haitian chants.

This is the place where the sun spends the winter, a subtropical haven that never sees the snow. Even in January, the coolest month, thermometers average around 74° Fahrenheit, while the trade winds temper the summer highs. With a good hat and the

The welcome's warm in Miami, resort city in the sun.

right lotions, you can enjoy this town all year round.

The city stands at the mouth of the Miami River on the shore of Biscayne Bay. Greater Miami's metropolitan area comprises 27 municipalities, which sprawl between the mysterious Everglade swamps and the Atlantic Ocean. The city's population tops two million—almost half of them of Latin American and Caribbean origin. Tallahassee runs Florida's state government and bureaucracy, but there's no doubt in anybody's mind that Greater Miami is the state's major centre for commerce, culture and sheer urban bounce.

For tourists, the city is most famous for the bright and breezy hotels of its resort area, Miami Beach, connected to the mainland by causeways. But massive construction at a cost of literally billions of dollars has given a dramatic new look to the downtown district, attracting business people and shoppers, as well as traditional tourists from the beaches. Sleek office towers line Flagler Street, Biscayne Boulevard and Brickell Avenue, the Wall Street of the South. Over 200 million dollars were spent on the South-east Financial Center alone,

tallest structure south of New York and east of Houston. With completion of the Bayside leisure complex and the ultra-modern "people-mover" (elevated train) system, renaissance in Miami has become a reality.

Yet a mere hundred years ago all was wilderness here. A handful of settlers traded with the Indians at the mouth of the Miami River, named by the Tequesta tribe to mean "Big Water". The pioneers lived in part by wrecking, salvaging the cargoes of ships that ran aground. They also farmed vegetables and citrus fruit for sale in northern markets. Sailing boats from Key West called every fortnight, bringing news of the outside world.

To this frontier outpost came a widow from Ohio named Julia Tuttle. Convinced of South Florida's potential for development, she urged railway magnate Henry Flagler to expand his Florida East Coast line south to Miami. At first the tycoon refused, but Mrs. Tuttle persisted. Finally in 1896,

Try rollerskating by the sea— even if you can't drink on wheels.

the railway reached Miami. Flagler built a luxury hotel on Biscayne Bay and Miami's course was set.

The resilient city has weathered killer hurricanes and financial collapse, the panic of the 1962 missile crisis and the usual modern big-city woes of riots and drug traffic, aggravated by a new influx of Caribbean refugees in the 1980s. The Miami authorities seem now to have their problems well under control.

Things are looking up for Miami Beach, too. Hugely popular in the 1920s and 30s, and again in the 50s and 60s, the resort is bounding back in favour as a new generation of holidaymakers discovers the pleasures of the "Florida Riviera", with its silver sands and swaying palms. Preservationists are restoring the Jazz Age hotels that line Ocean Drive in the Art Deco District, designated a national historic area. And the resort palaces along Collins Avenue are undergoing extensive remodelling.

The beach itself is bigger and better than before. The tide was lapping at the gateposts of the oceanfront hotels when the United States Army Corps of Engineers created a new strand stretching 300 feet to the highwater line. Now, as in the 20s, there's a boardwalk by the sea.

"Latins" are beginning to take to the charms of Miami Beach, but certain parts remain a largely Jewish enclave and retirement haven from the chills of the north. Black-suited rabbis walk the streets, deep in Talmudic discussion. And men in yarmulkas play cards by the hour, while their wives gossip over coffee and poppy-seed pastry, speaking Yiddish, Russian and occasional smatterings of English —justifying their inclusion among the city's "Anglos" (white residents of non-Hispanic ancestry). It's a scene described by Nobel Prize winner Isaac Bashevis Singer in his "Old Love" and other tales of Miami Beach life.

South of downtown, Little Havana provides a focus for Miami's thriving Hispanic community. The Spanish language dominates Calle Ocho, otherwise known to the mapmakers as South-west 8th Street. Cuban grocers display husked coconuts, bundles of sugar cane, piles of avocados, limes and plantains, mostly Dade-County grown. You can buy Brazilian leather goods, Mexican *piñatas*, Caribbean herbal cures and fat Havana cigars, hand-rolled in local factories. People from all over the city come to dine on shellfish and *lechón* (roast pork) in Calle Ocho's famous restaurants.

Taking their cue from the Cubans, some 40,000 Haitian refugees are transforming the area around 57th Street and N.E. 2nd Avenue into a Little Haiti. Restaurants and nightclubs with a Creole flavour and a French dialect are opening up and reaching out to a larger public. After years of economic hardship and political oppression back home, Haitians find America a welcome land of opportunity— and Miami is its gateway.

The city's most youthful neighbourhood is its oldest settlement: Coconut Grove, pioneered by a resolute band of New England intellectuals before the turn of the century. Yankee individuality has characterised the Grove ever since. Houses turn inward here, buried in lush vegetation, and huge, overarching trees shade bikeways and byways winding down to the bay. Sailing boats crowd the marina, and there are people everywhere, strolling around Florida's prettiest urban village, filling scores of streetside restaurants, open to the air.

East across the bay is the "Island Paradise" of Key Biscayne, home to Miami's perennial tourist attraction, the Seaquarium, and to the popular beaches of Crandon Park and Cape Florida. The University of Miami has its campus in the leafy glades of the city of Coral Gables, while Hialeah lays claim to its namesake, the most beautiful racecourse in the world.

Gambling on the horses, dogs and jai-alai games attracts a lot of people to Miami. Speedboat races, regattas, golf and tennis tournaments bring many more. But the great lure is the great outdoors and the myriad sports opportunities Greater Miami offers every month of the year: deep-sea fishing in the Gulf Stream, just a few miles offshore; snorkelling, sailing and windsurfing in the shallow waters of Biscayne Bay; superb swimming and waterskiing in the warm South Atlantic. Miami is a sportsman's paradise, with jogging, hiking and cycling for all.

Anyone who likes to shop will like Miami, the marketplace for Latin America. The Fashion District is the place to buy locally manufactured resort clothing and swimwear, while Design District shops **11**

stock the best in home furnishings from around the world. In recent years, most of the national department store chains have expanded their operations to the greater metropolitan area. Bloomingdale's is here, and Saks and Neiman Marcus—temples of affluence where a consumer society comes to buy, buy, buy.

Top attractions on the tourist circuit include the Sea-quarium of Flipper fame, and Miccosukee Indian Village, where the real natives of South Florida reside. Miami's own stately home, Vizcaya, is a must on any itinerary, as are the excellent shows at the Fine Arts Center. Nor is an excursion to the Everglades—that primeval world of grass and water—to be missed.

By way of an evening's entertainment, there's the glamour of a Latin supper club, or the glitter of a Miami Beach revue. An international roster

Calle Ocho mural mirrors life in Little Havana.

of a dozen different cuisines, from Cuban to kosher to Creole. Otherwise, the accent is on honest, American-style steaks and seafood and those great specialities of Greater Miami, sweet Florida stone crabs and creamy Key lime pie.

Perhaps the biggest event of the Miami year is the King Orange Festival and its climax on New Year's Eve, the King Orange Jamboree Parade, largest night-time march past in the world. On or near January 6, Little Havana stages its own annual Three King's Parade, complete with floats and marching bands. The Grand Prix motor race draws throngs of people to Biscayne Boulevard in February, and Carnaval Miami ushers in the Lenten season in exuberant, Latin style. A series of festivals highlights Miami's exciting cultural diversity; the Italian Renaissance Festival at Vizcaya, the Bahamas Goombay Festival in Coconut Grove, the Miami Greek Festival and Miccosukee Indian Annual Arts Festival.

Every year, Greater Miami is a magnet for six million tourists. And the number is rising as people from all over find fresh stimulation under the southern sun.

of jazz, pop and rock artists appears at Gusman Cultural Center, the Knight Center, Dade County Auditorium and other venues all over town. Avant-garde music and dance, opera, theatre, Broadway musicals—all receive an airing in Greater Miami.

Eating out means eating ethnic fare, sampling the best

13

Greater Miami at a Glance

Geography: Area 2,109 square miles, including 55 square miles of water, extensive farmland and Everglades swampland. The greater metropolis incorporates the cities of Miami, Miami Beach and 25 other municipalities.

Population: About 2 million (Anglo 43%, Hispanic 40%, Black 17%).

Climate: Winters are warm and sunny, summers hot and humid. Showers can occur late in the afternoon in summer.

Government: Each city has its own local government, which co-operates with the central metropolitan authority (Metro). The city of Miami is the seat of Dade County.

Industries: International banking and trade, tourism, agriculture.

A Brief History

About 4,000 years ago, Indians of Asian origin settled at the mouth of the Miami River. They had come to the end of a journey that brought them from Siberia to Alaska and on across the American continent. Wandering ever southwards, they arrived at last in a land of verdant forests and sunshine, rich in fish and game. And here they lived in splendid isolation until the white man came.

The Spanish explorer Juan Ponce de León discovered Florida in the spring of 1513. He called the peninsula *Pascua florida* after the feast of the flowers during the Easter season. Three months later, Ponce de León sailed down the coast to "Chequescha", the Indian settlement on the Miami River. No one knows for sure whether he stepped ashore, but from that time onwards the Spaniards referred to the Indians residing here as Tequestas.

This primitive yet resourceful people lived in platform houses built of cypress logs and palmetto thatch. They fashioned tools of conch shell and employed fish oil to repel insects. The Tequestas were hostile to the white man but less warlike than their neighbours, the Calusas, who attacked and mortally wounded Ponce de León on his return to Florida in 1521.

Territory of Spain

Subsequent attempts at exploration and colonisation failed, and Spain lost interest in Florida with the discovery of gold and silver in Mexico and Peru. In time, other European powers began to compete for territory in the New World. The French established an outpost in north Florida in 1562, but the Spanish soon ousted their rival. King Philip II appointed Pedro Menéndez de Aviles governor and charged him with extending Spanish influence throughout the peninsula.

As luck would have it, Menéndez met up with a fellow countryman on his arrival in Florida. Hernando d'Escalante Fontaneda had survived shipwreck to live with the Indians for 17 years. Versed in their language and their ways, he served as the governor's interpreter and guide. No sooner did Menéndez pay homage to the chief of the Calusa tribe than the Indian offered the Spaniard his sister in marriage. "Doña Antonía" became Florida's first convert to Christianity—and Menéndez de Aviles the first bigamist. The adventurer was married already to a noblewoman in Spain.

Having won the confidence of the Indians, Menéndez founded the city of St. Augustine (1567). That same year he established a mission at Tequesta under the auspices of a Jesuit lay worker, Brother Francisco Villareal. Some Spanish mutineers were already in residence when the Jesuit took up his post. Menéndez agreed to pardon them.

All went well for a while. Brother Villareal made a few converts, and the former mutineers constructed a simple fort. Menéndez himself turned up on a tour of inspection. After four days at Fort Tequesta, the governor left for Spain taking several Indians with him. It caused quite a sensation when he had the noble savages baptised in the cathedral of Seville. Back on the Miami River, the Spaniards clashed with the Tequestas. There were deaths on both sides before the Europeans made their escape. When the Indian entourage returned from Spain several months later, the mission was reopened, only to be abandoned again in 1570.

The British Take Over

In the long run, contact with the white man was the Tequestas' undoing. European diseases decimated the tribe, and those who survived fell prey to rum and marauding Creek Indians, pushed southwards into Florida by British colonial expansion.

In 1743, alarmed by Creek incursions and English raids, the Spaniards reactivated the fort and mission in south Florida—but not for long. The Tequestas drove them out. The remaining members of the tribe fled Florida for Cuba when Spain finally ceded the territory to England under the terms of the Treaty of Paris (1763). Creeks called Seminoles, or "wild ones", took possession of the land.

The British tried in vain to attract their countrymen to Florida. A few intrepid settlers arrived by boat from the Bahamas. Known as "conchs", they lived near the sea, which supplied their larder. "Crackers" travelled overland through Georgia to occupy the interior, where they grew collard and mustard greens, their staple diet. Both "conchs" and "crackers" stayed on when the territory reverted back to Spain in 1783.

Under Old Glory

Shortly after the United States annexed Florida in 1821, the population south of the Suwannee River stood at 317. Agriculture and the wrecking trade developed as settlements took shape at Key West, Indian Key and Cape Florida on Key Biscayne. In order to

Past of her people reflected in the face of a Miccosukee girl.

protect shipping, the U.S. government constructed a lighthouse at Cape Florida in 1826. About the same time, a Carolina planter named Richard Fitzpatrick imported **17** slaves to work a tract of land on the Miami River.

Sparsely settled though South Florida was, virgin land in the east was at a premium as the new United States extended its boundaries outwards across the continent. Congress therefore decreed that Indians remaining on the seaboard be transferred to reservations in the West. The Removal Act of 1830 had serious repercussions in Florida, sparking the long and bitter Second and Third Seminole wars*.

In December 1835, Indians massacred an army unit on manoeuvres between Tampa and Ocala. Seminoles in Miami took up arms a month later, murdering a family in residence on the Fitzpatrick plantation. They went on to burn the lighthouse at Cape Florida the following July.

The United States army sent troops to Miami in 1839, as Seminole raids continued. The soldiers were billeted at Fort Dallas on the Miami

Pioneers carved Miami from the tropical wilderness 100 years ago.

River, in barracks established by the navy a few years before. Chekika, chief of the tribe, personally led an attack on Indian Key which left seven dead. The soldiers at Fort Dallas vowed revenge. Dressed like Indians, they surprised Chekika in his Everglades hideaway, killing the chief and a number of his men.

But it was impossible to flush all the Seminoles out of the swamp. Bloodhounds were brought over from Cuba to stalk the Indians—a scheme that raised a cry of protest from people throughout the United States—but the dogs kept losing their way in the watery wilderness. The government finally gave up the fight in 1842, bringing the Second Seminole War to an inconclusive end.

That year Richard Fitzpatrick transferred his extensive Miami holdings to his nephew, William English. Filled with enthusiasm for the place, English mapped out a village he called Miami on the south bank of the river, advertising lots for sale for $1. The government offered free land to anyone who would hold it

---

* The Indians had already skirmished with American frontiersmen before Spain relinquished control of Florida. General Andrew Jackson himself rode victorious into the fray. He dislodged Seminoles from the north to the centre of the peninsula, opening new territory to development.

by force of arms for five years, and some stout souls carved out homesteads.

When Florida joined the Union in 1845, people predicted a brilliant future for Miami—until the Indians went on the warpath again in 1855.

Fort Dallas was expanded as a contingent of soldiers arrived to root out the recalcitrant Seminoles. Between missions, the men built roads and bridges in the wilderness around Miami. After two years of fighting, all but a few hundred Indians had been subdued. That small band withdrew deep into the Everglades as the Third and final Seminole War drew to a close.

Frontier Town

Deserters, spies and blockade runners frequented the Miami area during the Civil War (1861–65). Although Florida seceded from the Union, the state saw little bloodshed, and that little was confined to the north. New settlers arrived on the scene when peace returned, boosting the Dade County population to a grand total of 85 by 1870. One of them was William Brickell, who set up a trading post at the mouth of the Miami River. A new era opened as Indians returned to the Miami settlement to swap alligator skins, egret feathers and venison for beads, cloth, watches, spirits and the occasional treadle sewing machine. Meanwhile, thriving agricultural communities grew up at Lemon City, Coconut Grove, Buena Vista and Little River—hamlets that one day would be incorporated into the vast metropolis of Greater Miami.

In 1891 a wealthy widow named Julia Tuttle moved to town, setting up home in the rock house that William English had built. She became the biggest landowner in Miami, and over the next five years was instrumental in getting a rail link to the town.

On July 28, 1896, with a population of 343, the city was incorporated, taking "Miami" as its name. Streets were laid out, shops and hotels went up and the Bank of Bay Biscayne opened for business.

Resort City

No sooner had Miami taken shape than fire burned it to the ground. The blaze broke out early on Christmas morning, consuming 28 buildings. Luckily, Flagler's sumptuous Royal Palm Hotel escaped destruction. The five-storey, 350-room establishment opened on schedule in January, 1897, a portent of things to come.

Celebrities and notables like the politician Mark Hanna and meat-packing millionaire Philip Armour found

Julia Tuttle's Dream
Julia Tuttle was no ordinary pioneer but a visionary of the first order. She pronounced it "the dream of my life to see this wilderness turned into a prosperous country". Mrs. Tuttle confided her dream to railway tycoon Henry Flagler in 1892, entreating him to build his Florida East Coast line south to Miami. She even promised him the title to half her property. But Flagler was involved in the citrus industry in central Florida and in the development of luxury hotels at St. Augustine and Palm Beach. He simply had no time for new projects.

Two years later, chance played into Mrs. Tuttle's hands. Severe cold weather in the winter of 1894–95 destroyed the citrus crop in central Florida, while subtropical Miami remained free of frost. Mrs. Tuttle sent Flagler a bouquet of orange blossoms to prove the point, renewing her offer of land. Flagler accepted, and in April, 1896, the first train pulled into town.

the amenities to their liking, particularly the private yacht dock and swimming pool filled with crystal-clear bay water. Significantly, the hotel hosted its first convention that inaugural season, a gathering of the American Tobacco Growers. When the Royal Palm closed for the summer at the end of March, Miami was in the tourist business to stay.

On February 7 the following year—just as holiday-makers were returning to town for the winter—the *U.S.S. Maine* was sunk in Havana harbour, precipitating the Spanish-American War. More than 7,000 troops were sent to Miami as panic seized the city. In August, the conflict ended as swiftly as it had begun with the defeat of Spain. The incident brought Miami a lot of good publicity, focusing national attention on the locality and introducing some 7,000 potential visitors to the joys of life in the bayfront resort.

Things were barely back to normal when the sudden death of Julia Tuttle stunned the populace on September 14. She was 48. Everyone mourned the "Mother of Miami", whose persistence and perspicacity had brought their community into being. Mrs. **21**

Tuttle's son sold the family residence to an entrepreneur who turned it into a gambling casino, but the games of chance were for tourists only.

By 1910, Miami's population topped 5,000. The city had expanded south of the river along bayfront Brickell Avenue, called "Millionaire's Row" because of the profusion of imposing houses. Miami boasted telephones and cars, a fire station, hospital, cinemas and schools. The city had become a sea port, linked to the Atlantic by Government Cut, a channel dredged to a depth of 18 feet.

The continuation of the Florida East Coast Railway to Homestead and Florida City opened the South Dade pinelands to agriculture. Construction of the final stretch, to Key West, was Henry Flagler's final achievement. A year after the track was completed in 1912, the "Father of Miami" died at the age of 82. Other dreamers would come along to take his place.

On the Oceanfront
Miami Beach was the haunt of crocodiles when John Collins established an avocado farm beside the sea. As a sideline, the 70-year-old horticultur-

22 ist founded the Miami Beach Improvement Company. He initiated land sales and began construction of a bridge to the mainland (1912). Work advanced rapidly—until Collins ran out of cash. People called the bridge "Collins's Folly". They thought the man had gone mad. At the crucial moment, an entrepreneur from

A bayfront landmark since 1916, palatial Vizcaya brings European flair to the Florida Riviera.

Indiana named Carl Fisher put up all the capital needed in exchange for a wide swath of oceanfront land.

Fisher had plans of his own for Miami Beach. He cleared away the palmettos and mangroves and went on to create new acreage by dredging the shallow bay. While war raged in Europe, "America's Winter Playground" took shape, **23**

complete with golf courses, tennis courts and polo fields. The U.S. declaration of hostilities halted construction for a while, but business activity picked up quickly once the armistice was signed on November 11, 1918.

Boom and Bust

In an era of easy money and changing moral values, people flooded into Miami and land sales boomed. Developer George Merrick sold the first lot in his "Master Suburb" of Coral Gables in 1921. At first it seemed an unlikely venture —the site was so far from town—but within a year Gables property transactions totalled an unprecedented $1,400,000.

As demand for land increased, plots six and eight miles beyond the Miami city limits fetched prices of $20,000 an acre and more. Bay sites slated for reclamation were sold "by the gallon", and some salesmen didn't bother with land at all. Speculating on spiralling prices, they traded in "binders"—five or ten per cent deposits paid in advance of final sale.

Jet-skier (and architecture) make
24 *waves on Biscayne Bay.*

Some unscrupulous estate agents gave the area a bad name, further blackened by the rising incidence of crime, some of it prohibition-related. The situation got so far out of hand by 1925 that the Ku Klux Klan offered to step in and keep the peace. City officials politely declined.

The boom was already losing momentum when a devastating hurricane visited its fury on Miami in September, 1926. Not a building escaped unscathed, with damage running to millions of dollars. Townspeople were still picking up the pieces when the stock market crash of 1929 triggered the Great Depression. Scores of local businesses went bankrupt and every Miami bank but one defaulted.

Boom Again

Recovery came earlier to Miami than most American cities, thanks to tourism and the expanding aviation industry. (Both Pan American Airways and Eastern Airlines had begun to operate out of Miami.) During the 1937–38 season alone, around 800,000 visitors holidayed there. To accommodate all the people, hundreds of hotels went up in streamlined style on the south shore of Miami Beach, in the area known today as the Art Deco District.

War and its Aftermath

World War II brought big changes to Miami. The air force and navy opened military training camps in Miami and Miami Beach, and by the end of the war, one soldier in four had received basic training here. Golf courses and beaches were turned into drill grounds, and hotels were commandeered as barracks. No less important was Miami's role as a staging area for missions to China and India.

Furnished with government loans, many former servicemen returned to the Greater Miami area in the late 1940s and early 50s, purchasing homes in the city they had come to know during the war. As the suburbs burgeoned, new hotels like the Fontainebleau and Eden Roc opened on Miami Beach, once again a fashionable holiday spot.

Since the 50s, the suburbs have expanded. Miami's international airport has developed into the country's second busiest, cruise ship traffic has built up and Greater Miami has mushroomed into one of the most sophisticated resort capitals in the world.

Landmark Events

c. 2,000 **B.C.**	Indians settle at the mouth of the Miami River.
A.D. 1513	Juan Ponce de León discovers Florida.
1567–70	Jesuits maintain a mission at Tequesta on the banks of the Miami River.
1763	Spain cedes Florida to England.
1821	The United States annexes the territory of Florida.
1826	Cape Florida Lighthouse goes into operation.
1835–42	Second Seminole War pits the U.S. Army against Florida's Indians.
1842	William English offers land for sale in the village of Miami.
1845	The territory of Florida attains statehood.
1855–57	Indians subdued in Third Seminole War.
1861–65	Deserters, spies and blockade runners swarm to Miami during the Civil War.
1870	Dade County boasts 85 inhabitants. William Brickell sets up a trading post in Miami.
1896	The arrival of the railway in April opens Miami to development. The city is incorporated on July 28.
1898	U.S. troops are sent to Miami during the Spanish-American War.
1910	Miami's population grows to 5,000.
1915	The city of Miami Beach is incorporated.
1921	Land boom begins.
1926	A severe hurricane leaves 100 dead, 850 injured and thousands homeless. Property values fall.
1929	Following the Stock Market Crash, Miami banks default and businesses go bankrupt. Great Depression sets in.
1930s	Recovery begins early for Miami. Art Deco hotels go up on Miami Beach.
1940–45	The city serves as a military training camp and staging area in World War II.
1950s on	Suburbs expand. New hotels open up on Miami Beach.

What to See

Greater Miami combines the pleasures of resort life with all the urban excitement a tourist could wish for. From a base by the seaside—be it Key Biscayne, Miami Beach, Surfside, Bal Harbour or Sunny Isles— it's easy to make forays across the bay into the greater metropolis.

There's no better introduction to Miami than a ride on the Metrorail, the elevated public transport system. The line crosses every ethnic and economic boundary in the city as it travels from suburban

South Dade to the centre and on through Miami's northern neighbourhoods.

We begin our tour of Greater Miami "downtown", in the city of Miami, the expanding business and cultural hub of the metropolitan area. After a look at the bay front, port and Brickell Avenue

financial district, we enter the Cuban enclave of Little Havana. Then it's on to the "City Beautiful" of Coral Gables and trendy Coconut Grove, a Floridian Greenwich Village. There's just time for a taste of bohemia before we cross over to the Beaches: the lush isle of Key Biscayne, glamorous, garish Miami Beach, friendly Surfside, exclusive Bal Harbour, popular Sunny Isles.

The scene changes abruptly as we head out through the southern suburbs to the pineland and hammocks of Everglades National Park, where signposted footpaths penetrate deep into the tropical wilderness. To reach the northern sector of the park, we return to town and follow Tamiami Trail west past the hamlet of Coopertown (centre for airboat rides) to Shark Valley in the open glades, scene of biking, hiking and tram expeditions, water levels permitting. Last stop on our Everglades itinerary is further down the Trail: the reservation of the Miccosukee Indians, who shun the con-

Ride the downtown Metromover—not for commuters only.

crete and glitter of the encroaching metropolis for a life nearer nature.

We propose other sightseeing possibilities grouped by kind—tourist attractions like the Seaquarium and Parrot Jungle, historical sights that include The Barnacle and Cape Florida Lighthouse, museums such as Vizcaya and the Historical Museum of South Florida. Choose from our selection according to your interests, referring to the map on pages 32 and 33.

Casual, charming Coconut Grove— just one of Miami's urban villages.

Greater Miami

There's a lot of territory to cover on the Miami mainland, beginning with the reviving city centre.

Downtown

A generation ago, residents abandoned Miami proper for suburbia, and the city fell into decline. Now the focus of urban life is shifting back to the centre. If you think of downtown as an area to avoid, you're decidedly out of date, though local people will forgive the misconception. Miamians themselves have hardly had time to get used to the changes that have transformed the central business

Getting Around

At first glance, Miami seems a confusing urban sprawl, crossed by a bewildering profusion of expressways. On closer acquaintance, the logic of the town plan becomes clear. Laid out on a grid, Miami divides into four sections: north-east, north-west, south-east, south-west. Flagler Street in the city of Miami serves as the boundary between north and south. Miami Avenue is the crossroads between east and west. The eastern quadrants of town cover a relatively small area, while the western sections have expanded out towards the Everglades—far beyond the limits foreseen by Miami's pioneers. Addresses will be easier to find if you remember that an avenue, place or court runs north-south, and that a street, terrace or alley has an east-west orientation.

Outside rush hours (7 to 9 a.m. and 4 to 6 p.m.), the expressway system speeds cross-town journeys. The main north-south arteries include the North-South Expressway (also known as Interstate-95, or I-95), which travels from the south-west section right through the city and on up the state. The Palmetto Expressway, sometimes referred to as State Road (SR) 826, goes from South Dade to North Miami. The Florida Turnpike Extension (SR 821), links Homestead and Florida City to northern Dade County. For through journeys, it's best to avoid the congested national north-south highway, US 1, known locally as the Dixie Highway.

For east-west trips, take the Dolphin Expressway (SR 836), which runs just south of the airport to the North-South Expressway, or the Airport Expressway (SR 112), which connects the terminal to Miami Beach via the Julia Tuttle Causeway.

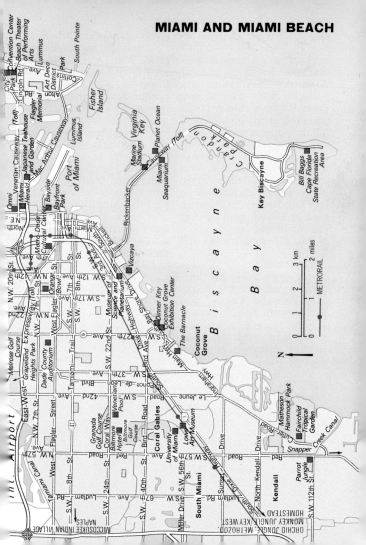

MIAMI AND MIAMI BEACH

district out of all recognition.

Construction and congestion make it difficult to drive downtown. Parking can be a problem, too. You'll save yourself a lot of trouble if you ride to the centre on Metrorail (all the outlying stations have car parks), transferring to the downtown **Metromover** at Government Center. This computerised adjunct to the metropolitan transport system loops around the urban core of Miami, with its concentration of high-rise office blocks, shopping arcades and hotels.

You'll come close to some of the city's lofty new landmarks, including the **Southeast Financial Center**, seat of the Southeast Bank. Lunchtime concerts are held in the airy plaza, an urban meeting place designed for Florida living.

You can try out your Spanish on cosmopolitan **Flagler Street**, main thoroughfare of the downtown district. The neighbourhood is predominantly Latin, and so are the merchants who offer competitively priced jewellery, clothing and electronic goods for sale to shoppers from south of the border, enhancing
34 Miami's reputation as the marketplace of the Americas.

Among the big stores and small shops of East Flagler stands the **Gusman Cultural Center**, a 1920s pastiche of Spanish Baroque architecture. Now a venue for concerts and plays, the centre began life as a music hall. Stand-up comics and variety acts always played to a full house, for the Gusman was one of the first air-conditioned buildings in the city: ice under the floorboards kept the place cool.

Miami's love affair with Spanish architecture continues at the **Metro-Dade Cultural Center** (1979), further on at 101 West Flagler. That master of post-modernism, Philip Johnson, designed the nostalgic stucco and tile structure in collaboration with John Burgee. Three institutions flank a central courtyard: the main branch of the **Miami-Dade Public Library**, largest in the south-east; the **Center for the Fine Arts**, providing gallery space for some superb travelling shows; and the **Historical Museum of South Florida**, featuring lots of "hands-on" exhibits (see pp. 67–68).

Office towers spike the skyline where the Miami River meets Biscayne Bay.

The Miami Melting Pot

For a long time, Miami was as southern as grits and fried chicken. Just about everybody spoke with a drawl in the city they called "Miamah".

After World War II, northerners and mid-westerners swelled the "Miamee" population. Coming from diverse backgrounds, the newcomers included many Jews of Eastern European origin who brought a taste for borscht and bagels with them.

The arrival of hundreds of thousands of exiles from Cuba in the 1960s and 70s added yet another element to the ethnic equation, as Cuban coffee and black beans took the city by storm.

These days, immigration from Nicaragua, Colombia, Venezuela, Ecuador and other Central and South American countries is reinforcing the Latin influence, while thousands of Haitians are introducing a Creole flavour into the ethnic stew.

The inauguration of the **James L. Knight International Center** in 1982 set the seal on Miami's reviving fortunes. Situated at the mouth of the Miami River, the centre incorporates a hotel, exhibition hall, meeting rooms and indoor sports arena. There is no more historic site in the city than this. Here the Tequesta Indians established a settlement 4,000 years ago, and here Spanish missionaries came to convert them in the 16th century. Here, too, stood the William English house and the barracks of Fort Dallas, founded during the Third Seminole War. Finally, on this spot, lived Julia Tuttle, remembered as the "Mother of Miami".

A **River Walk** leads from the Knight Center along the north bank of the Miami River, and there are plans to extend the promenade out around the bay. For the moment, you can stroll in sight of the Riverparc Hotel and the yellow wood-frame **Flagler House**. Erected around 1898, this railwayman's dwelling is a venerable Miami monument. Not far away, **José Martí Riverfront Park** offers modern docking facilities and another waterside walkway. Away from the river, playing fields and a swimming centre cover ten urban acres.

Boat yards, marine suppliers and industrial installations border the murky Miami River as it winds east through the city from the Everglades. Clean-up crews have their work cut out for them, but the river is reviving. And after a

Courtyard café at the Omni—one of Miami's cool, urban spaces.

long absence, cargo ships have returned to the waterway.

At the junction of the Miami River and Biscayne Bay rise the travertine marble towers of **Miami Center**, a hotel, shopping, office and condominium complex. In 1895, Julia Tuttle ceded the property to Henry Flagler, who built his luxury hotel, the Royal Palm, on this spot. The opulent Hotel Intercontinental continues that grand tradition.

The older downtown hos- **37**

telries overlook **Biscayne Boulevard**, with its central island of palms. This sweeping thoroughfare is the scene of the Miami Grand Prix, contested by champions of the motor-racing world. The boulevard also plays host to the King Orange Jamboree Parade, a New Year's Eve event since 1936.

The Great Escape

They call it Miami's number one fun day afloat. Leave town before breakfast and you have the whole morning ahead of you—to indulge in a leisurely buffet breakfast, swim, sunbathe, meet new people. SeaEscape packs all the pleasures of a longer cruise into one very full day.

Join in the parties and competitions. Work out in an exercise class. Play the slot machines. Try your luck at bingo or roulette—and it's still only time for lunch. After a lavish meal, the ship docks at Freeport in the Bahamas for an afternoon of sightseeing, beaching or shopping. You'll have plenty of time to look over the duty-free bargains in china, silver and perfume at the International Bazaar—and the Bahamian handicraft in the straw market next door—before the ship lifts anchor for Miami and an evening of entertainment on board.

Across the way, the green expanse of **Bayfront Park of the Americas** edges Biscayne Bay. For years motorists sped by with little more than a glance at the palms and shrubbery, or the John F. Kennedy Torch of Friendship, a symbol of goodwill between the United States and its neighbours to the south. That was before the **Bayside Market Place** started building on 20 acres of park land. In the tradition of London's Covent Garden and Boston's Faneuil Hall, the new centre will comprise a host of small shops and restaurants around a central square. By way of added attractions, *H.M.S. Bounty* is to be moored offshore. Built by Metro-Goldwyn-Mayer for the 1962 feature film *Mutiny on the Bounty,* this three-masted barque is an authentic replica of the merchant ship that carried Captain Bligh and Fletcher Christian to the South Pacific in the 18th century.

A causeway leads across the water to the Dodge Island premises of the Port of Miami, "Cruise Capital of the World". Over two million passengers a year set sail from Miami aboard a fleet of 20 vessels that includes the 70,202-ton *Norway,* biggest cruise ship in the world. An innovator in the cruise business, Miami pioneered the one-day **SeaEscape**, bringing cruising within the reach of all.

Further up the boulevard stands Freedom Tower, a relic of the 1920s modelled after the Giralda tower in Seville, Spain. Designed for the *Miami Daily News,* the 17-storey edifice acquired its present name during the Cuban exodus, when the Refugee Center had headquarters here.

Beyond Bicentennial Park, you pass the entrance to scenic **MacArthur Causeway**, which cuts across Watson Island on its way to Miami Beach. There's a great **view** of the port from the island. On any given day, a score of tankers and huge, ocean-going liners lie at anchor, dwarfing a passing parade of pleasure craft.

Back on the mainland, the offices of the *Miami Herald* extend along the bayfront from the MacArthur to the Venetian causeways, in sight of the manmade islands of the Venetian chain. Just opposite, the concrete bulk of Plaza Venetia reflects in the mirror of the bay. This self-contained skyscraper block boasts its own marina, restaurants and shops. A skywalk connects the

Building on Sand

A dozen artificial isles grace Biscayne Bay: the Venetian Islands, the Sunset group, Palm, Star and Hibiscus islands. The by-product of channel dredging operations, these geometric strips of land provide the maximum of waterfront footage.

Carl Fisher refined the dredging procedure on Miami Beach (which is itself three-quarters fill). Beginning in 1913, his machines scooped up material from the bay bottom, including decaying animal and vegetable matter, and turned it into dikes. The stench was terrific. But Fisher discovered that the odour disappeared as the soupy material solidified. Rich, black soil could then be spread over the sand, and trees planted to retain the land.

The islands in the bay have been secluded retreats for personalities as diverse as Howard Hughes and Al Capone. The gangster acquired his grand, Spanish-style house at 93 Palm Island in 1928, shortly before the St. Valentine's Day Massacre. Indicted for income tax evasion several years later, Capone was forced to abandon the palm trees for prison. He returned to Miami on his release in 1939. And he lived here until he died, eight years later—of natural causes.

Marriot Hotel at Plaza Venetia to **Omni International** in Biscayne Boulevard. A suburban-style shopping mall transplanted to the city centre, Omni has all the requisite department stores, chain concerns and fast-food outlets, plus cinemas, child-care facilities—and a luxury hotel for good measure.

Developed for commerce during the Depression, the northern stretch of Biscayne Boulevard retains many low-rise structures from the 1930s. They alternate with purpose-built office blocks like the blue-and-white tile headquarters of Bacardi International, the rum company. Stop off at the **Bacardi Art Gallery** (2000 Biscayne Boulevard), where a changing succession of contemporary art shows attracts a discerning public weekdays.

Miami's financial district lies south of the Miami River in the area of **Brickell Avenue**. The title "Wall Street of the South" is no exaggeration: in recent years, nearly 100 international banks specialising in foreign transactions have opened offices here. While New York trades with Europe, an ocean away, and Los Angeles deals with the distant Far East, Miami has an expanding market with Latin

America right at its doorstep.

South of Brickell, the graceful mansions of an earlier era share the coastline with luxury high-rise condominiums like the Atlantis, Imperial and Palace. If the new Miami has a symbol, it is the blue rectangle of the **Atlantis** with its 12th-storey sky court, featuring a free-form jacuzzi, full-grown palm tree and high-tech stairway to the stars. The critics call it "Beach Blanket Bauhaus".

Over in Little Havana, dominoes is the only game in town.

A stately old structure dominates the southern bayfront: **Vizcaya**, the Italian-Renaissance-style mansion completed in 1916 for James Deering, scion of the International Harvester family. Purchased by Dade County in 1952, the house with its fabulous furnishings is open to the public daily (see p. 65).

Little Havana

For Americans from the heartland, Little Havana is as foreign as Paris or Rome. The language, the food, the customs—all couldn't be more different. Here in the Cuban enclave, the Latinisation of Miami is complete.

Little Havana covers a 3½-square-mile section of the city, bounded roughly by West Flagler Street and Coral Way, I-95 and 37th Avenue. Although tourists are un- **41** doubtedly drawn to the neighbourhood, it's not a tourist attraction, but a vital centre of Hispanic life. Anglos and Cubans alike patronise the supermarkets, bakeries and fruit stands, the shops for records, shoes and clothing. Bilingual schools, Spanish-language cinemas and bespoke tailors all have premises in this lively community of 200,000 residents.

The business district centres on S.W. 8th Street, better known as **Calle Ocho**, a one-way thoroughfare that runs from west to east, linking Coral Gables to the downtown district. After a coffee at one of the streetside counters, stop to watch the chess and domino games in **Antonio Maceo Park**, at the crossing of 14th Avenue. Cuban women may have entered the work force, but they have yet to penetrate this male preserve filled with cigar smoke and the clicking sound of the playing pieces.

On the opposite side of the street, a mural depicts the patron saint of Cuba, the *Virgen de la Caridad* (Our Lady of Charity). In the 17th century, she appeared to three mariners of Cuba in a vision, saving them from shipwreck—or so the story goes.

Coral Gables

Winding streets, sweeping lawns and some gracious Mediterranean- and colonial-style homes make the affluent Gables a model of suburbia. Citizens aglow with health and well-being jog, cycle and play golf and tennis in a setting of shade trees and ornamental fountains six miles from downtown. Founded in 1925, the "City Beautiful" was America's first planned community.

Discreet signs bearing the words "Coral Gables Self-Guided Tour" direct visitors to points of interest around town. Ask for a map of the route in City Hall, the colonnaded construction of 1928 at the crossing of Le Jeune Road, Biltmore Way, Coral Way and Miracle Mile. Amazing mainly in name, the Mile is the principal shopping street of Coral Gables.

Follow Coral Way to **Coral Gables House**, childhood home of Gables developer, George Merrick. The city takes its name from this coral rock residence of 1906 with a gabled roof of red barrel tiles (see p. 78). A few streets away at **Venetian Pool** in De Soto Boulevard, arched footbridges and arcaded buildings reflect in the waters of an artificial lagoon. Originally a

The South Pacific meets the Adriatic at Venetian Pool.

quarry for the coral rock used in early Gables construction, the pool was transformed from eyesore to beauty spot by George Merrick. During the boom, swimming competitions featuring Esther Williams and Johnny Weissmuller brought the crowds out to Coral Gables. People have been coming ever since, attracted by the cascades, grottoes and small sand beach of "the world's most beautiful swimming hole".

The most prominent building around, the towering **Biltmore Hotel** (Anastasia Avenue) was the last word in luxury accommodation and resort facilities during its pre-war heyday. Guests enjoyed unlimited access to the golf courses, polo fields and tennis courts on the premises. And when the charms of America's largest swimming pool palled, there was always the private beach on the bay front, reached by gondola via an artificial waterway.

The romance began to fade after the 1926 hurricane left South Florida in a shambles. Now the city of Coral Gables has restored the old Spanish-Moresque-style hotel to its former magnificence. The renovated country club building adjacent houses a restaurant

and the **Metropolitan Museum and Art Center** (see p. 66).

From modest beginnings in the 1920s, the **University of Miami** (off US 1) has developed into a leading centre of learning, known internationally for its School of Marine and Atmospheric Science. The **Lowe Art Museum** in the university grounds presents some good temporary exhibitions, in addition to an excellent study collection of Renaissance and Baroque painting (see p. 66).

South along the bayfront, Coral Gables encompasses **Matheson Hammock,** 560 acres of mangroves, live oaks, nature trails, picnic areas, boat docks and beaches. Neighbouring **Fairchild Tropical Garden,** an Eden of orchids, ferns and palms, is one of the most popular horticultural attractions in the United States (see pp. 69–70).

Coconut Grove

Augustus St. Gaudens and Alexander Graham Bell had homes in the Grove. American writers James Whitcomb Riley, Robert Frost and Ten-

Paved bikeways make the going good in the Grove.

On the Key Biscayne bayfront, sea and sky come together in a sunset panorama.

nessee Williams did a lot of work here. Hip in the 60s, trendy in the 80s, the freewheeling Grove is Miami's bohemia.

Coconut Grove embraces the bayfront from S.W. 32nd Road to Battersea Road, extending inland to US1 and Le Jeune Road. Absorbed by an expanding Miami in 1925, the Grove is an urban village within the city limits.

People from all over converge on the village centre, where dozens of small shops offer clothing, jewellery, pottery and the ethnic arts. Weekends and evenings the traffic can be chaotic as crowds jam the sidewalk cafés and garden restaurants along **Main Highway**, **Commodore Plaza** and **Fuller Street** in the heart of the Grove. Choose a table early or reserve in advance—it's standing room only here after dark. Even at the best of times driving can be difficult in Coconut Grove. You'll see more if you explore by bike or on foot.

A showcase for good theatre, the **Coconut Grove Playhouse** stands at the crossing of Main Highway and Charles Street, where Dade County's first Black settlement grew up. A State Historic Site lies directly opposite: **The Barnacle,** first home on the bay (see p. 76).

It's a short walk under the banyans to **Plymouth Congregational Church,** just off Main Highway in Devon Road. A

Grove landmark since 1917, the vine-clad coral rock edifice looks positively timeworn. In the grounds stands the Grove's original schoolhouse, a one-room wood-frame affair knocked together with timber salvaged from shipwrecks. Main Highway runs into McFarlane Road, which leads past grassy Peacock Park to the bay. A plaque in the park marks the location of Peacock Inn, Dade County's first hotel (1882).

Packed with hundreds of sailing boats, **Dinner Key Marina** is a picturesque spot. In the old days picnic parties rowed out from the harbour **47** for lunch or dinner, which accounts for the name. Site of a U.S. naval air base during World Wars I and II, Dinner Key was also home to the flying clippers of Pan American Airways in the 1930s. Right on the bay, the Art Deco terminal building is being converted into a museum of aviation, while the old hangars serve as the Coconut Grove Exhibition Center, scene of the annual boat, dog and home shows.

Joggers, roller skaters and fitness fanatics are thick on the ground at **David Kennedy Park,** which occupies an attractively landscaped sweep of bayfront land. Across South Bay Shore Drive, a luxury line-up of hotels overlooks the water—the Grand Bay, Mutiny and Coconut Grove. Joining their ranks is the select Mayfair House, a hotel of suites in Virginia Street.

The hotel adjoins the exclusive shopping and recreation compound of **Mayfair-in-the-Grove.** With gushing fountains, lush foliage and designer boutiques galore, Mayfair is a cross between the gardens of the Alhambra and the Champs-Elysées arcades. Leave your car with an attendant in the underground garage.

The Beaches

From Key Biscayne to Sunny Isles, the blue Atlantic laps Miami's shores. The oceanfront has always been a great recreational asset, attractive to tourists and residents alike. In the old days, ferry boats provided access to the sea. Now a series of causeways spans Biscayne Bay, connecting the mainland to the Beaches.

Key Biscayne

So many Miamians converge on this "Island Paradise" at weekends that the city had to erect an 85-foot bridge to accommodate all the traffic. Residents are resigned to the crowds. You can't keep people out of paradise.

The English explorer, John Cabot, sighted Key Biscayne in 1497. Juan Ponce de León followed him here in 1513. The Spaniard called the island *Santa Marta,* but the Indian name survived: "Biscayne" is a corruption of *Bischiyano,* "The Favourite Path of the Rising Moon". A military base during the Second Seminole War, Key Biscayne later became the resort of wreckers and then of hunters and fishermen.

A few escapists built homes

on the island in the early years of the century, but development came only with the opening of Rickenbacker Causeway in 1947. Thanks to extensive parkland at the north and south of the island, Key Biscayne retains an aspect of natural beauty rare in metropolitan Miami.

It's a long, leisurely ride across the water to the island. Early in the day, the causeway beaches fill up with windsurfers and water-skiers. Sun-bathers bask on top of their cars. Be sure to spare a glance for Miami's evolving skyline, visible in the middle distance; you can always pull off the road for a lingering look on the return journey.

Crossing Virginia Key (Key Biscayne's sister isle), you pass **Miami Marine Stadium,** venue for power boat races, summer

Jaws revisited: monster of the deep bares teeth at Planet Ocean.

concerts and other open-air events. Next comes **Planet Ocean,** a science attraction featuring film shows and didactic displays (see pp. 74–75). Flipper the dolphin and Lolita the killer whale cavort for the crowds at the **Seaquarium,** just opposite. The shows are continuous, so no matter when you arrive you'll be on time for one of them (see p. 75). Alongside the Seaquarium stands the University of Miami's Marine Science Laboratory. The proximity of the two institutions is more than coincidental, for they cooperate in the study of underwater life.

Another stretch of causeway brings you to Key Biscayne itself. Dozens of sailing boats lie at anchor in **Crandon Marina,** painting the bay waters red, yellow and blue. Tufted clouds overhead echo the convolutions of the mangroves. Pelicans and gulls perch on the piers.

On the ocean side of the island, the 2½-mile public beach of **Crandon Park** attracts more than a million people a year, from swimmers and sunbathers to Frisbee players. Barefoot joggers head south along the beach past the big hotels and condominium blocks to historic Cape Florida, also accessible by bikeway and road. And there's always a procession of walkers just taking it easy.

Crandon Boulevard leads through the unassuming town centre to the **Bill Baggs Cape Florida State Recreation Area,** 406 wilderness acres covering the southern tip of the island. Here the waters of the Atlantic meet those of Biscayne Bay. You can picnic among the pines or fish from the low retaining wall along the bay shore. Out in Biscayne Channel is Stiltsville, a colony of holiday homes built on pilings.

Cape Florida's ocean beach is half as long as Crandon Park's—and twice as popular. At weekends and on public holidays it can get so crowded that the entrance gates have to be closed early in the afternoon. But most of the time Cape Florida is the peaceful haunt of sea birds. In the nesting season, ponderous turtles struggle across the sand to lay their eggs.

The old **Cape Florida Lighthouse** dominates the southern beach front. Several times a day, park rangers guide visitors around the site.

There's a place in the sun for everyone on Miami Beach.

Go for a swim and come back for a fascinating tour of inspection (see pp. 76–78).

Leaving the park, you can turn off towards **Hurricane Harbor,** on the bay, for a quick spin through former U.S. president Richard Nixon's old neighbourhood. Don't look for the former winter White House, though; it has long since been knocked down.

Miami Beach

For a lot of people, Miami means the Beach—the resort island that is America's most durable winter playground. The famous hotels stretch for seven oceanfront miles from Government Cut to 87th Street. They include stream-lined survivors from the 1930s and peerless monuments of 50s kitsch. For a time after World War II, more luxury hotels were constructed in Miami Beach than in the rest of the world combined. With the advent of jet travel and package holidays, the area fell out of favour. Now business is picking up again as a younger crowd frequents the Beach.

MacArthur Causeway enters the island at 5th Street, near the expanded **Miami Beach Marina.** Fishing charters operate from this public facility, which incorporates nautical shops, a waterfront restaurant and an outdoor café. The neighbourhood is the oldest on the Beach. Re-development has claimed most of the early landmarks, although **Joe's Stone Crab Restaurant** in Biscayne Street still stands its ground. A Miami Beach institution since 1913, Joe's narrowly escaped demolition when buildings in the area were razed to make way for South Pointe, a hotel, office and condominium complex. **South Pointe Park,** a new centre of leisure and recreation, covers 17 waterfront acres at the very tip of Miami Beach.

North of 6th Street, the **Art Deco District** offers architecture—and more. Preservationists involved in the restoration of this national historic area invite you to return to the tropical 30s. The setting is compelling: 800 buildings in distinctive Deco style line the streets of a square-mile zone stretching up to 23rd Street. The concentration of Deco architecture is the greatest in the world. Buildings sport sunbursts, waves, palm trees and flamingoes: fantasy meets futurism on Miami Beach.

You can join a **walking tour** of the district, organised by the Miami Design Preservation League on Saturday mornings at 10.30. The starting point is league headquarters, 1236 Ocean Drive.

To see what restoration has done for the district, call in at one of the Art Deco hotels, on the sea in **Ocean Drive**—notably the streamlined Leslie, Carlyle and Cardozo, where wrap-around windows frame sweeping views of the sea, and jazz music plays softly. Attractive to the young and nostalgic, these properties have been upgraded at a cost of $12 million, breathing new life into the area.

Away from the sands, the world of Deco embraces commercial **Washington Avenue,** a mosaic of supermarkets, delicatessens and bakeries. Posting a letter is less of a chore in the Moderne surroundings of

Miami Beach Moderne: Art Deco with a southern accent.

FONTAI

the Miami Beach Post Office at No. 1300, while further up the street a sizable congregation worships beneath the Middle Eastern domes of Temple Emanu-El, a late Deco monument of 1947. The presence of a couple of Cuban restaurants and food shops along Washington highlights the changing ethnic character of the area.

True to its name, **Espanola Way** recreates the atmosphere of a Spanish village. Constructed before the streamlined craze swept Miami Beach, this ensemble of Mediterranean-Revival buildings is in the process of con-

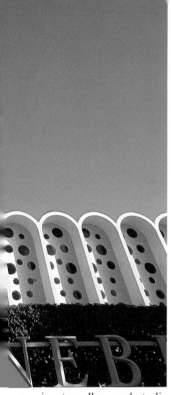

Architecture turns heads on Miami Beach.

version to gallery and studio space. At the far end of Espanola, you come to expansive **Flamingo Park,** the haunt of tennis players day and night.

Artists and craftsmen are also moving into **Lincoln Road Mall,** the street they called the "Fifth Avenue of the South". Open-air trams still circulate along the pedestrian thoroughfare with its low-rise Deco shop fronts, but most of the old glamour is gone.

Housed in an elegant 30s structure of coral rock, the **Bass Museum** in Park Avenue **55** is a bastion of culture on the Beach. In addition to an eclectic permanent collection, the museum organises some timely exhibitions (see pp. 66–67). Jazz concerts on Sundays bring out the devotees of Deco.

On the periphery of the Art Deco District is that busy facility, the **Miami Beach Convention Center,** and the 3,000-seat **Theater of the Performing Arts.** A lot of people prefer to approach the Beach just west of here, via the Venetian Causeway and Dade Boulevard.

The rambling **Miami Beach Boardwalk** begins at 21st Street and runs out along the water, behind the big hotels, as far as 46th. The rustic wooden walkway made an immediate hit when it opened in 1984. Covered pavilions provide a place to sit and contemplate the panorama of sea and sky. "No Skating, No Dogs", warn the signs. The beach itself is something of a phenomenon: 300 feet wide, it stretches to infinity.

Arthur Godfrey Road swoops from Julia Tuttle Causeway across the Beach to the heart of **hotel row.** Time was, when at least one new luxury hotel a year opened in this part of Collins Avenue. Now the street is built up all the way to Sunny Isles. There's the Seville, Sans Souci, Versailles, Barcelona... the sweep of concrete seems inevitable, as much a part of the landscape as Indian Creek or the ink-blue Atlantic.

Revamped for the 80s, the fabulous **Fontainebleau Hilton** continues to lord it over them all. People wander in for a look at the free-form pool with its grottoes and cascades —the slick new symbol of a reviving Miami Beach. For nostalgia seekers, the Boom Boom Room and Poodle Lounge are still going strong more than three decades after Morris Lapidus gave this monument to the world. Next comes the extravagant **Eden Roc** and, beyond that, the popular **Doral on-the-Ocean.** For a faithful clientele, the legend of the Beach lives on at the Doral.

Condominiums proliferate in the northern reaches of Collins, a mecca for retired New Yorkers. Yachts tie up along Indian Creek, and there are some great golfing greens in the area, like the municipal Normandy Shores course on **Normandy Isle.** The 79th Street Causeway provides a direct link to the mainland by way of North Bay Village.

The Beach Communities

Eight streets long, the friendly village of **Surfside** is popular with French Canadians—so popular that the community organizes a "Salute to Canada" festival every year in March. Families of all nationalities are attracted by Surfside's pleasant beach, reasonable hotel rates and informal air.

The desirable resort community of **Bal Harbour** lies farther north along Collins. (It's also accessible from the North Miami mainland by Broad Causeway.) De luxe hotels crowd the oceanfront, within hailing distance of **Bal Harbour Shops,** a luxury mall in an attractive garden setting of orange trees, palms and shrubbery.

Ranged over two landscaped levels, Neiman Marcus, Bonwit Teller and Saks Fifth Avenue join forces with some of the best-known names in international fashion—Gucci, Mark Cross, Charles Jourdan, Cartier, Yves Saint-Laurent and Guy Laroche to list just a few.

Out in the car park, uniformed guards in pith helmets keep a watchful eye on all the Mercedes and Rolls-Royces.

Beyond Bal Harbour, Collins crosses popular **Haulover Beach Park,** a Metro-Dade facility. There's swimming along a two-mile stretch of sand (ocean currents can be strong), fishing from an 1,100 foot pier, plus golf and tennis —even deep-sea fishing by charter craft from the Haulover marina. You can also board an excursion boat for a tour of Biscayne Bay and other points of interest in Greater Miami.

Collins leads on to **Sunny Isles,** famous in the 1960s as a magnet for singles and swingers but more sedate these days. (The Sunny Isles Causeway runs directly from North Miami Beach—on the mainland, despite the name —to the resort.) Fishermen make for the pier at the junction of the causeway and Collins, a kaleidoscope of coffee shops, delicatessens, restaurants, bars, clubs—and motels.

Motel Row stretches for two miles or so along the ocean side of the street. The theme motels are architectural classics of the pop era: the Tahiti has a Polynesian motif; the Sahara sports stucco camels. The very names hold out the promise of more, much more, than sun and sea: Mandalay, Aztec, Monaco, Suez, Hawaiian Isle.

The Everglades

It's not an accessible landscape. There are no majestic peaks, just an awesome flatness, relieved by dense tufts of hardwood hammock—islands of green in the "River of Grass". Silence enfolds you. Plumed clouds drift in an empty sky. Here in the Everglades you luxuriate in space and quiet.

Everglades National Park covers the southern tip of Florida, an area of more than 2,000 square miles. The Everglades region is vaster still, extending as far as Lake Okeechobee. A sheet of water 50 miles wide flows southwards from the lake to Florida Bay and the Gulf of Mexico. It moves imperceptibly through that flat, flat terrain that slopes just as imperceptibly downwards.

In summer and autumn —the rainy season—the water level in this great conduit rises, though much less now than formerly. Decades of drainage and "water management" have dried out the glades, upsetting the fragile balance of nature. Concerned citizens propose restoring the free flow of water in order to "Save Our Everglades".

Like Mt. Everest, the Serengeti Plain and Galapagos Islands, the Everglades is a World Heritage Site. The pinelands, hammocks and sawgrass prairie shelter some of the rarest birds and animals

Glades Guidelines

- Mosquitoes and other biting insects can be annoying, above all in summer. Wear a hat, loose, long-sleeved shirt and trousers. Use plenty of repellent—and no perfume. It attracts mosquitoes as honey does bees.
- Don't approach birds or animals or attempt to feed them. Alligators, in particular, appear deceptively lethargic.
- Avoid contact with toxic plants, like poison ivy, poisonwood and manchineel.
- Beware of poisonous snakes: water moccasins, coral snakes, diamond-back and pygmy rattlesnakes.
- Swimming is prohibited. Alligators and water moccasins lurk in freshwater ponds; crocodiles and barracuda cruise offshore waters.
- To hike off the trails, apply at one of the Visitor Centers for a back-country permit.
- Freshwater fishing is allowed in designated areas with a licence.
- Pets are banned from nature trails and amphitheatres.

58

on earth, including the great white heron and southern bald eagle, the Florida panther, crocodile and Everglades mink. More than 40 kinds of plants are unique to the area.

The best time to visit the park is winter or spring, when the concentration of animal and bird life is at its greatest —and when insects are at their least bothersome. Everglades National Park remains open 24 hours a day, all year round. There are two access routes from Miami: south-west via the Turnpike Extension and Route 9336 to the Main Entrance (35 miles), and west 25 miles along Tamiami Trail (US 41) to Shark Valley, open to pedestrians, cyclists and tram passengers only.

You'll see a much larger section of the park if you take the south-westerly route, but a trip to Shark Valley can be combined with a visit to Coopertown and the Miccosukee Indian Village.

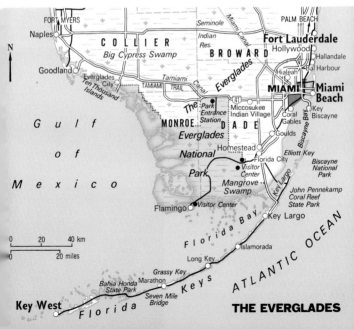

THE EVERGLADES

The Road to Flamingo

Before you go into the park, stop at the **Main Visitor Center** to see the excellent 15-minute introductory film on the Everglades prepared by the National Park Service. Don't forget to pick up a free map and information about organised activities.

A road runs 38 miles from the entrance to Flamingo on Florida Bay. All along the way, turn-offs lead to viewing areas where raised platforms, boardwalks and signposted footpaths take you safely into the wilderness. If time is short (half a day or less), concentrate on the Gumbo Limbo, Anhinga and Pa-hay-Okee Overlook trails, which offer the most in the way of landscape and wildlife close to the entrance.

Off the main road to the left, the **Gumbo Limbo Trail** makes a half-mile circuit through a hammock, or tropical forest, of mahogany, wild coffee and native gumbo limbo trees. Plaques identify the vegetation. They call the gumbo limbo the "tourist tree" because its bark turns red and peels. The poisonwood tree looks as noxious as it is: hideous orange spots cover the trunk like a canker. Early in the morning and late

at night, otters, raccoons, opossums—even bobcats and white-tailed deer—wander this way. But the witching hour comes late in the afternoon, when pinpoints of light shine diamond-bright through the dense canopy of leaves.

The nearby **Anhinga Trail** swings out across the saw grass and over a slough, or freshwater channel. This is the best place in the park to view animals and birds at close quarters. You'll come across

alligators, marsh rabbits, egrets and, of course, anhingas.

On the **Pineland Trail** you penetrate a dense stand of tall, slender-shafted Dade County pines, habitat of the rare Florida panther. Fifty years ago, much of Dade County looked like this.

Across Rock Reef Pass (altitude three feet), the **Pa-hay-Okee Overlook Trail** offers an intimate view of the saw grass prairie that Marjory Stoneman Douglas describes in her Florida classic, *The Everglades: River of Grass*. Although "Pa-hay-Okee" means

A is for Anhinga

The Anhinga Trail takes its name from a curious bird with a snake-like neck and tail feathers that resemble a turkey's. Alas, poor anhinga, its oil glands are not sufficient for its needs. The bird gets literally soaked to the skin when it dives into the water, and it has to hang itself up to dry.

"River of Grass", the saw grass is not a grass, but a sedge—an older and more primitive plant form. Grasses abound at Pa-hay-Okee, too: arrowhead, Muhly grass, Everglades beardgrass.

Past more halting places—Mahogany Hammock, Paurotis Pond, Hell's Bay (hell for canoers), Nine Mile Pond—you come to **Flamingo,** centre for fishing, hiking and boating expeditions. Rooms at the inn, as well as self-catering cottages and campsites, are very much in demand in the winter season, so try to book ahead. The marina supplies everything from bait and tackle to fully equipped houseboats for hire.

A memorial outside the Visitor Center honours Guy Bradley, an Audubon warden who died here in the line of duty in 1905. He was killed by poachers hunting egrets for their feathers, a practice outlawed in 1903 as the species neared extinction. Look through one of the telescopes on the breezeway and you'll see descendants of the birds he gave his life to save, preening themselves just offshore in their protected rookeries.

A sunset cruise of Florida Bay is the perfect way to end an Everglades day.

Exploring the Trail

About 15 miles from Miami, Coopertown is home to the Kennon clan, operators of the original Everglades **airboat ride,** one of Florida's transcendent tourist experiences. From first light into the night, the Kennons will take you through canals teeming with alligators, where huge sheafs of saw grass sheer up out of the water and white birds flap darkly in the sky.

Airboats can travel in as little as half an inch of water, opening up areas of the glades that no conventional motor craft could reach. When water levels allow, you'll cross the saw grass prairie to hammocks that attract egrets, herons, ibis and the elusive purple gallinule, an iridescent beauty that pads about on clumsy yellow feet—rather like an elegantly dressed woman in training shoes.

Further along the Trail, the walk-in gate at **Shark Valley** remains open round the clock. You can trek up to 15 miles on the Loop Road to the Everglades Observation Tower or stroll in leisurely fashion to Bobcat Hammock, Otter Cave or Heron View, where wading birds like the roseate spoonbill are wont to gather. Two-hour, ranger-led tram tours depart every hour in season.

The Miccosukee tribe of Indians claims the Everglades as its homeland. Reduced by war and removal to a band of 50 souls, the tribe now numbers 500. Like the better-known Seminoles, the Miccosukees are a branch of the Creek nation, but while the Seminoles speak the Muskogee language, the Miccosukees converse in Mikasuki. (The tongues are mutually unintelligible.) The Miccosukees continued to follow a traditional life-style until the 1920s—longer than any other tribe in the United States. Even now they strive to preserve their identity and their traditions.

The big attraction at the **Miccosukee Indian Village** is the alligator arena, where muscular braves wrestle mean-looking reptiles in daily shows. Like bull-fighters and motor-racing drivers, they're nonchalant about the dangers of their chosen sport. A tour of the village involves craft demonstrations, like basket weaving and patchwork, and a look at the artefacts in the small museum.

Rare look at a purple gallinule.

A couple of Indian families actually live on the premises, taking up residence in their cool, thatched "chickees" when the last of the tourists go home. However, most of the tribe live down the road in a little suburbia of frame and stucco houses, with the Everglades for their back garden.

Another amenity of the neighbourhood is the **Great Cypress National Preserve,** just across the way. The biggest of the bald cypress trees here have seen 700 summers.

Miami's Miccosukees call the Everglades home.

Museums

Don't miss **Vizcaya,** magnificent former residence of tractor millionaire James Deering, on the bay at 3251 South Miami Avenue. The Italian Renaissance-style mansion incorporates some precious architectural elements: pink marble gateways from the Palazzo Bevilacqua in Verona, a carved stucco ceiling from the Palazzo Rossi in Venice, and an Adam mantelpiece from Rathfarnham Castle in Dublin.

Deering personally acquired it all. Not the typical captain of industry but a cosmopolite equally at home in France and the United States, he had an exquisite and highly developed sense of style. Deering's health was already failing when the house reached completion in 1916. Eight short years were left to him to enjoy his creation.

Dade County purchased the estate and 30 acres of hammock in 1952. The Deering heirs contributed the original furnishings, including Ferrara tapestries from the collection of Duke Ercole II, a 16th-century trestle table with a Farnese provenance and a handsome Neapolitan bed that belonged to Lady Hamilton, paramour of Lord Nelson, England's great admiral.

Volunteer guides conduct tours of the house at frequent intervals throughout the day. Restoration work permitting, you'll see every nook and cranny, from the imposing Renaissance Hall to the tiny Rococo telephone room and wood-panelled lift—Neoclassical tour-de-force of the Otis Elevator Company.

Lush formal **gardens** descend to the bay. Like the hill gardens of Italy, they contain statuary, fountains, hidden grottoes and a casino, or place of retreat. Deering commissioned Gaston Lachaise to carve the birds on the Peacock Bridge, and he entrusted the figures on the stone barge (a breakwater) to the skills of the leading sculptor of the day, A. Stirling Calder, father of the more famous Alexander.

In Deering's time, the charming North Italian Farm Village across South Miami Avenue supplied Vizcaya with poultry, fruit and vegetables. The one-time Superintendent's House has been renovated to display the **Claire Mendel Collection** (50 S.W. 32nd Road) of 15th- to 19th-century painting and sculpture (open weekends only). The works of art were **65** donated to Vizcaya by a citizen of Miami Beach.

Check the local newspapers for details of travelling exhibitions periodically on view at the **Metropolitan Museum and Art Center,** 1212 Anastasia Avenue in Coral Gables. Chinese and Pre-Columbian works of art are highlights of the small permanent collection.

Special shows and lectures attract the general public to the University of Miami's **Lowe Art Museum,** off US 1 at 1301 Stanford Drive in the Gables. The Lowe also houses the Kress Collection of Renaissance and Baroque art, an important cultural resource for Miami, with works by Lippo Vanni, Andrea della Robbia, Lucas Cranach the Elder and others. Miami is one of 18 U.S. cities to benefit from the philanthropy of Samuel H. Kress, founder of the Kress chain of five- and ten-cent stores.

Situated in a quiet residential neighbourhood of Little Havana, the **Cuban Museum of Arts and Culture** (1300 S.W. 12th Avenue) organises exhibitions and events with a Latin accent. Shows feature members of the Cuban vanguard in exile, including the "Miami Generation" of artists who came of age in the United

States. This is one of the most vital institutions in Miami, dedicated to preserving Cuba's cultural traditions.

The **Bass Museum** (2121 Park Avenue) brings some stimulating travelling exhibitions to Miami Beach. In 1964, Austrian-born entrepreneur John Bass and his wife, Johanna, presented most of the works of art on permanent display. Bass bought what he liked: a selection of European paintings, sculpture, Orien-

Vizcaya—from millionaire's mansion to museum.

tal bronzes and ecclesiastical vestments. Docents, or volunteer guides, will point out the highlights.

The **Black Archives** (5400 N.W. 22nd Avenue) display photographs and documents from a cache of historical material relating to Miami's Black community. The archives are also involved in the preservation and revitalization of the Overtown neighbourhood. Contact staff for information about tours, cul-

tural activities and special events (tel.: 638-6064).

The **Historical Museum of South Florida** has premises downtown in the Metro-Dade Cultural Center (101 West Flagler Street). Displays recall 10,000 years of history in the area, beginning with the geological events that shaped the land. The outstanding single **67** exhibit is a rare, double-elephant folio of Audubon's *Birds of America,* valued at more than $1 million. Tequesta artefacts take pride of place in the American Indian section, one of the largest in the United States. And audio-visual presentations dramatise episodes from the more recent past—19th-century anthropologist Clay MacCauley's encounter with the Miccosukee tribe and Ralph Middleton Munroe's experiences as a Coconut Grove pioneer. The Coral Gables Trolley will transport you back to the 1920s, when everybody in Miami had land fever. But the most haunting relics are those of yesterday, a somewhat shabby Mercury space capsule and a Haitian refugee boat that somehow made it to shore in 1979.

Across the courtyard, the **Center for the Fine Arts** is the venue for some excellent travelling shows.

Attractions

You may not have time for all of them, but you'll certainly want to take in a few. Make your choice from the list below.

Biscayne National Park (Homestead). This marine preserve covers 175,000 acres of water and land in Biscayne Bay, including Elliot Key and 23 attendant islets. Boat tours open up the underwater world, a sanctuary for sea creatures large and small, including manatees and turtles, stone crabs, spiny lobsters and shrimps. Park rangers are on hand to provide commentaries and answer questions. They also conduct nature walks on Elliot Key, site of a rare tropical hardwood forest. Bring along plenty of insect repellent—the mosquitoes are voracious. Write or telephone for information and reservations: P.O. Box 1369, Homestead, Florida (tel. 247-PARK). Or contact the Biscayne Aqua-Center (see p. 117).

Fairchild Tropical Garden (10901 Old Cutler Road, Coral Gables). Exotic plants, trees and flowers from around the world thrive in this bayside botanical showplace. There are hundreds of varieties of palm alone, including the African oil palm, South American honey palm, the smooth-trunked Bailey palm and the petticoat palm, skirted with fronds. In a glade of their own grow the palm-like cycads, plants that flourished in the Cretaceous Period, when dinosaurs stalked the earth. Water cascades through the Rare Plant House, steamy

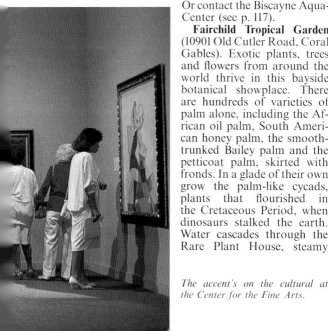

The accent's on the cultural at the Center for the Fine Arts.   **69**

shelter for orchids, bromeliads and a profusion of ferns, while sprinklers make up for any shortage of water in the rain forest. Go for a circuit of the garden by tram or join a guided walking tour for more leisurely exploration.

Gold Coast Railroad Museum (S.W. 152nd Street and S.W. 124th Avenue). You'll see some historic rolling stock, including the glass-domed observation car of the Chicago-to-San Francisco *California Zephyr* and the *Ferdinand Magellan,* one-time private Pullman car of the President of the United States. Custom-fitted with steel armour plating, bulletproof glass and two escape hatches, the *Magellan* has a brass-railed platform at the rear from which the head of state could declaim. At weekends, the museum takes tourists for a ride on a vintage train pulled by an old Seaboard steam engine.

Hialeah Park Race Course (E. 4th Avenue). The horses pound the mile-and-a-half oval at Hialeah only two months a year, either in January and February or March and April. The rest of the time, the track opens its gates daily to tourists. You can visit the grand French-style clubhouse,

formal gardens, paddock area and backstretch with stables for 1,500 thoroughbreds. Hialeah's famous pink flamingoes fly over the infield every afternoon. Born at the track, the birds never stray far from their native turf.

Children under the age of 18 are not allowed at race meetings, but they are welcome to breakfast in the clubhouse at weekends, when a commentator is on hand to talk about the horses as they exercise.

Metrozoo (S.W. 152nd Street and S.W. 124th Avenue). This cageless facility is one of the most progressive zoos in the world. Animals compatible with the South Florida climate live in surroundings that closely approximate their natural habitat: white Bengal tigers prowl around a replica of a 13th-century shrine at Angkor Wat. African grazing animals lope across a miniature facsimile of the Serengeti Plain. And hundreds of South-East Asian birds soar through an imitation rain forest in the free-flight aviary. The best way to see Metrozoo is by tram or on foot. Don't miss out on the elephant rides, trained bird show and wildlife talks.

Monkey Jungle (14805 S.W. 216th Street). Some 500 primates call the treetops and jungle paths of this commercial attraction home. The cages here are for the visitors; the orang-utans, gorillas, baboons, gibbons and others wander at will. Shows take place several times a day: trained chimps look cute for the tourists' cameras in the Monkey Theatre, and Java monkeys or crab-eating macaques—"the skin-diving wild monkeys"—demonstrate their underwater skills in the Monkey Swimming Pool. Watch your fingers: these monkeys can bite.

Museum of Science (3280 South Miami Avenue). The "hands-on" exhibits here show various phenomena of nature in action, from the refraction of light to the generation of electricity. Popular with school groups, the

Bumper crop of coconuts at Fairchild Tropical Garden.

Don't miss the beasts at the Metrozoo, or the birds at the Parrot Jungle.

museum presents slide shows, films and live demonstrations, including glass-blowing and dissections. Ask for an "explainer" to take you round.

Orchid Jungle (26715 S.W. 157th Avenue, Homestead). Walk the jungle trail of one of the world's largest outdoor orchid gardens and observe technicians in the modern Plant Tissue Culture Laboratory, where orchids are cloned in a science-fiction setting of test tubes and centrifugators. The Orchid Jungle sells plants and seed (fine as face powder) and provides information and professional expertise to growers around the country.

Parrot Jungle (S.W. 57th Avenue and S.W. 112th Street). Articulate and numerate, the birds at the Parrot Jungle sing, laugh and cry,

count forwards and backwards, add and subtract. Watch them perform in daily shows repeated every hour and a half. Afterwards you can wander through 20 acres of hammock where more birds fly free. A total of 74 different species are on show—1,100 birds in all. Aviaries house some of the more exotic, like the great billed parrot from the Molucca Islands, the Patagonian conure and the green Amazon parrot. The macaws on the giant perches by the entrance provide the ultimate photo opportunity. Let them pose in pairs on your arms and shoulders for Miami's classic tourist shot.

Pennekamp Coral Reef State Park (US 1, Key Largo). Named in honour of John Pennekamp, a *Miami Herald* reporter who championed the preservation of South Florida's coral reef, this underwater preserve lies to the south of Biscayne National **73**

Park. Glass-bottom and snorkel boats ferry visitors six miles out to Molasses Reef for a fascinating look below water.

Planet Ocean (Rickenbacker Causeway). Most of the exhibits at this ocean-oriented attraction invite participation. Push a button and you set the Gulf Stream in motion, its course symbolised by thousands of coloured lights. Walk through the weather engine and you feel the power of hurricane-force winds. Children love to touch the seven-foot "iceberg", but to adult eyes the big block of ice more closely resembles the carved centrepiece of a Miami hotel buffet. However, the nautical exhibits are authentic enough: the Perry-Link Deep Diver, the original yellow submarine; and the tiny *April Fool*, small-

Flipper rises to the occasion at the Seaquarium.

est sailing boat ever to cross the Atlantic. Less than six feet long, the truncated wooden vessel looks like half a ship.

Seaquarium (Rickenbacker Causeway). Don't miss film-star Flipper in a live appearance. The dolphin frolics with some fishy friends on the original set of the Flipper movies, preserved for posterity at the Seaquarium. Lolita, the lovable five-ton killer whale, goes through her paces in the Whale Bowl, while Salty the

sea lion takes centre stage in a marine magic show. For their part, the man-eaters in the shark channel do what comes naturally as they lunge—most convincingly—for bloody hunks of fish flesh. A sign nearby warns, "Danger! Hungry Live Sharks". And so they are.

You'll want to look in on the manatees, or sea cows, including Lorelei, the first to be conceived and born in captivity (1975). That leaves thousands of species more to discover—the denizens of the Reef Aquarium and some two dozen wall tanks in the Main Aquarium.

Southern Cross Astronomical Observatory (on the roof of the Museum of Science). You can behold the Miami moon through a 14-inch Celestron telescope or a Clark antique of 1900. The observatory is open free of charge in the evening at weekends and on Sunday afternoons, when the sun is under scrutiny.

Space Transit Planetarium (3280 South Miami Avenue). Multi-media shows alternate with astronomy programmes and laser spectaculars (lights and rock music). For information about current offerings, call the Cosmic Hotline, 854-2222.

75

Historic Sights

Progress is erasing Miami's past, but a few monuments remain from that not-so-distant time before the railway, when Indians and alligators had the run of the place.

The Barnacle (3485 Main Highway, Coconut Grove). On a stretch of shoreline redeveloped with condominiums, The Barnacle survives from the era of the bay. Naval architect Ralph Middleton Munroe built the wood-frame structure in 1891 with timber salvaged from shipwrecks. When his family later outgrew the place, Munroe simply jacked the structure up and added a second floor underneath. Electricity was supplied in 1913, and plumbing was installed in the 20s. Occupied by the Munroes until 1973, the house has been returned to its original appearance.

Florida park rangers open The Barnacle to visitors each week from Wednesday to Sunday. You'll have to join a group to take a look round. The times of tours are shown at the entrance gate.

Photographs of old Dade County taken by Ralph Munroe decorate the sitting room, filled with dark wood furniture and a collection of books.

Upstairs, the dining room has built-in cabinets modelled on those of a yacht, and the breezy bedrooms display articles of clothing and memorabilia.

In the open attic at the top of the house you'll see an early "air conditioner"—a skylight with a series of windows which can be opened and closed to create suction and drive out hot air. The system devised by Munroe is so effective that architects in the fuel-efficient 80s are adapting it for modern use.

Some 2½ acres of virgin hammock screen the house from Main Highway. Sable palms, live oaks, gumbo limbo and mahogany trees luxuriate on the high land of The Barnacle. Down by the bay stands Ralph Munroe's boathouse and the shallow-draught *Micco,* designed by Munroe the same year as the house. The craft broke records in 1892 when it sailed to New Jersey in six days.

Cape Florida Lighthouse (Bill Baggs State Park, Key Biscayne). By local standards, this structure of 1825 is more than venerable. Indians attacked the lighthouse during the Second Seminole War. Damaged in the skirmish, the tower was later raised to a height of 95 feet. At the beginning of the Civil War, supporters of the Confederacy destroyed the lantern. It was restored and used until 1878, when a new lighthouse was built further out at sea. Reactivated exactly 100 years later, the Cape Florida light guides small craft into the Cape Florida channel.

The prolific Australian pines introduced into the island as a windbreak have been cleared from the neighbourhood of the lighthouse. In their place grow the inkberry plant, which provided Indians with war paint and settlers with ink; the sea grape, used to make wine and jelly, and the coontie, or arrowroot plant, a source of starch.

The New-England-style keeper's house was reconstructed from photographic evidence in 1968. Furnished simply, with wooden tables and chairs, rag rugs, trundle bed and patchwork quilts, it has an air of pioneer authenticity. After a look at the interior, you'll have ample opportunity to inspect the old

Hurricane Watch

An average of ten hurricanes a year spawn in the Caribbean and South Atlantic, but few of these violent tropical storms ever reach land. You're unlikely to experience a hurricane. Miami hasn't been hit by a storm since 1964.

A hurricane is a doughnut-shaped vortex of wind that revolves around a calm centre, or "eye", at speeds of 75 miles an hour or more. Measuring anything from 60 to several hundred miles in diameter, it moves at about 15 miles an hour.

The most destructive hurricane to hit Miami this century struck in September of 1926. Raging winds, waves and rain lashed the city for eight hours before the storm abated. Believing the worst to be over, people emerged from their houses as the eye of the hurricane passed overhead—only to be caught up in its fury again. When the force of the winds reached 128 miles an hour, measuring devices blew away along with the roofs of many buildings. More than 100 people died and around 850 suffered serious injury.

These days, sophisticated tracking systems give people plenty of time to batten down and take shelter. When the weatherman announces a "hurricane watch", it means a storm may be heading towards the coast. A "hurricane warning" is given 24 hours before the storm is expected to hit. **77** lighthouse. An iron stairway spirals upwards to a viewing platform in the lantern. Those who make it to the top will be rewarded with a dizzying panorama of turquoise seas and sugar-white sands—Cape Florida as Ponce de León knew it.

Visible from the beach, the historic lighthouse site is accessible only from the state park. Rangers admit visitors every day except Tuesdays. Ask at the park entrance about tour times.

Coral Gables House (907 Coral Way). This coral rock dwelling was the only house for miles around when the pioneering Merrick family moved in at the turn of the century. Many of the original furnishings are on view, together with memorabilia of the Coral Gables Plantation, a grapefruit concern operated by George Merrick's father, Solomon, a retired Congregational minister.

Life here was cosy for the Merricks, who imported their Pianola and devotional books to the Florida frontier. Merrick spent the evening hours perusing *Fox's Book of Martyrs,* while his wife, Althea, worked at her needlepoint and dabbled in oils. Paintings by Althea and her youngest son, Richard, decorate an upstairs bedroom, as well as oils by her brother, Denman Fink —hired by George Merrick as artistic adviser to the city of Coral Gables. The municipal charter was signed out in the garden, under the shade of a spreading rubber tree.

Coral Gables House is open to the public on Wednesdays and Sunday afternoons.

Coral Castle (US 1 and 286th Street). Promoters tout this South Dade landmark as a cross between Stonehenge and the Great Pyramid. An immigrant from Latvia named Edward Leedskalnin built the coral rock house, as well as its solid rock furniture and monolithic sculptural groups, singlehanded between 1920 and 1940.

He was a frail man, no more than five feet tall, yet somehow he managed to excavate, carve and position huge blocks of coral rock weighing from six to 30 tons each. Leedskalnin never allowed anyone to see him at work, and to this day no one can quite figure out how he did it.

Spanish Monastery Cloisters (16711 West Dixie Highway, North Miami Beach). While shopping in Europe for art works in the 1920s, William Randolph Hearst picked up this 12th-century building at a bargain price of $50,000. He thought it would make a nice setting for his swimming pool at San Simeon. The cloisters were duly dismantled, the stones packed in straw and shipped to New York in 10,000 numbered crates.

With foot-and-mouth disease raging in Spain, the U.S. Department of Agriculture ordered the crates opened and the straw—a possible source of contamination—destroyed. During the operation many of the stones were returned to the wrong crates. Hearst consigned "the greatest jigsaw puzzle in history" to a warehouse for the next 25 years.

In 1952, two Miami entrepreneurs reassembled the Early Gothic structure. The Cuban tile floors are modern (somebody forgot to pack the original ones), and the armorial corbels are antique replacements. Otherwise, the cloisters are authentic in every way, down to the well in the patio and the wrought-iron gate at the entrance to the gardens.

The episcopal diocese of South Florida holds church services here on Sunday and Wednesday mornings. At other times the cloisters are open to tourists.

What to Do

The resort metropolis offers tourist activities of all kinds, although the beach comes first for most people, with a little shopping and nightclubbing on the side.

Sports

Virtually every warm-weather sport is catered for here. The resort hotels all have swimming pools, tennis and shuffleboard courts. A few maintain golf greens on the premises.

Water Sports

Bay beaches are best for windsurfing and water-skiing, ocean beaches for swimming. For an up-to-the-minute weather report, including full details of wind, sea and sun-tanning conditions, call the Weather Line: 976-1010 (24-hour service).

Swimming. Although right of way to the beach may be private, the shore is public property to the highwater line. Ease of access makes Miami Beach popular with Miamians. Try the swinging 21st Street Beach or the expansive swimming area at 46th, set right in the middle of the great resort hotels. There's a **79**

place in the sun for the public at 53rd, 64th and 72nd to 74th streets. North Shore Open Space Park Beach (79th to 87th streets) has the most elaborate facilities, with Vita course, boardwalk and thatched shelters in an attractive setting of palm trees and sea grape. Possibilities further north include the beaches at Surfside, Bal Harbour and Sunny Isles.

Key Biscayne's beaches are the clear favourite of local swimmers and sunbathers. Crandon Park has snack bars, picnic facilities, a bath house and cabanas to let by the day, week or month, while Cape Florida provides plenty of picnic tables and grills under the pines.

Jellyfish, Portuguese man-of-war and sting rays can present a hazard to swimmers on Atlantic beaches, but they won't bother you if you leave them alone. In the rare event of a man-of-war invasion (usually after a heavy storm), life guards advise swimmers to keep out of the water.

Outstanding among municipal swimming centres is historic Venetian Pool in Coral Gables (see pp. 43–44).

Windsurfing. The most popular spot in town is off Rickenbacker Causeway, between the toll gate and Seaquarium, followed by Dinner Key. Some hotels and half a dozen specialised dealers rent equipment.

Water-skiing. If your hotel doesn't have boats or skiing gear, you can fit yourself out at one of the ski centres along the Rickenbacker and 79th Street causeways. For a real thrill, try jet-skiing around the bay.

Surfing. The biggest rollers come in to shore at South Pointe and Haulover Beach.

Boating. Oceanfront hotels generally have a flotilla of catamarans and sunfish sailing boats for hire, while several firms at Dinner Key in Coconut Grove and at the Miami Beach Marina rent sailing boats by the hour, half-day, day and week. If you've never sailed before, the protected waters of Biscayne Bay make a good place to learn. Most hire companies advise beginners to complete at least six hours of instruction before going out alone.

Motor boats are available at Pelican Harbor Marina on the 79th Street Causeway, Crandon Marina on Key Biscayne and Flamingo Marina in Everglades National Park.

Canoeing is popular in the Everglades, but some trails

require more skill than others—notably Hell's Bay and the Wilderness Waterway. You can rent a canoe by the hour at the Flamingo Marina, although Everglades Canoe Outfitters, just outside the national park entrance, offers the most complete service.

Snorkelling. Mask and flippers open up an exotic underwater world of sponges, sea whips and soft corals, spiny lobsters, crabs and rainbow-bright tropical fish. At the northern limit of Florida's coral reef, Biscayne National Park is the best place to snorkel in Dade County. Unless you're experienced, stay on the patch, or fringing reefs, close to shore: currents can be strong on the outer barrier reef. Hire a boat and skipper it yourself or join an organised excursion aboard the *Reef Rover III* (see p. 117).

Snorkellers and divers must display a warning flag while they are below water. It is illegal to remove coral from the sea bed.

Scuba-diving. You can dive down to a wreck in Biscayne National Park, or explore the shallow reefs off Key Bis-

Boating is a way of life in maritime Miami.

There's plenty of sand to occupy the bucket and spade brigade.

cayne. Other likely places include the waters around Fowey Rock, Elbow, Pacific and Carysfort lighthouses. Various shops rent equipment, arrange for tuition and organise excursions.

Fishing. You can fish the bay waters from causeways and bridges where catwalks are provided, or cast your line into the Atlantic from beaches or piers like the popular ones at Haulover Beach Park and Sunny Isles. As for deep-sea fishing, you can charter a private boat or join a group of fishermen on a "party boat" for a reasonable fee per person (rods provided for a small extra charge). For the names of charter companies, private and group, look in the *Yellow Pages* under "Fishing Parties".

Other Sports

There are endless possibilities for active participation throughout the year in Miami.

Golf. The municipalities and Dade County Parks and Recreation Department alike maintain a number of popular public courses, including the scenic Key Biscayne Golf

Links—voted Florida's best public course. Certain clubs, like the famous Doral, open their greens to non-members. Although not every hotel has a course of its own, many can arrange for their guests to play at a private club. For further information on golfing, consult the brochure "Golf is Greater in Miami", available from the Greater Miami Convention & Visitors Bureau.

Tennis. With more than 400 courts in the metropolitan area, Miami is indeed tennis country. Apart from all the hotel courts, you can play at any of a number of public tennis centres, including Flamingo Park in the Art Deco District and North Shore Open Space Park.

Cycling. More than 130 miles of paved bike paths make the going good in Miami. You can sightsee by bike on Key Biscayne, where shady paths cross the island. Ride out to Fairchild Tropical Garden or the Parrot Jungle from Coconut Grove along the banyan-lined path that parallels Old Cutler Road. Or combine birdwatching and bike riding at Shark Valley in the glades (see pp. 62–63).

Jogging. You can do it in a park—David Kennedy in the Grove is a local favourite—barefoot on the beach or, if you don't want to get your toes wet, along Miami Beach's oceanfront boardwalk.

Hiking. Everglades National Park is the place to go. Join a group or strike out on your own. Ask at the Visitor Centre about nature trails and back-country destinations.

Hunting. Turkey shoots are a Coopertown speciality. So is frogging, strictly a nighttime occupation. The Kennons will provide you with a gig, head lamp and their considerable expertise (see p. 62).

Spectator Sports

In sports-mad Miami, you can telephone for the latest news and scores 24 hours a day, revised every ten minutes. Dial 976-3300.

Motor Racing. The Miami Grand Prix in February attracts the best drivers on the international circuit. The race is run on the six-lane sweep of Biscayne Boulevard and in Bicentennial Park downtown.

Horse Racing. Hialeah Park (see p. 70) and Gulfstream, in Broward County, share winter dates on a rotating basis. North Miami's Calder track opens for the summer season. Established in the 1920s, Hialeah has a thoroughly patrician air. Calder, by contrast, **83**

is newer and more functional, but the track can still produce champions. A recent Kentucky Derby winner, Spend-a-Buck, started out here.

Dog Racing. Dog races are held every evening, in addition to several matinées a week. Biscayne Kennel Club in Miami Shores and Flagler Dog Track in the city of Miami open in turn.

Jai-alai (pronounced "high lie"). At the Miami Jai-Alai Fronton near the airport in N.W. 37th Avenue, you can put bets on—or just watch—this exciting, fast-paced ball game from Spain's Basque country. Helmeted players use long-handled, scooped, basket-like *cestas* to hurl and catch the ball as it ricochets at fantastic speed around the three-walled court. Games take place every night except Sunday, and on certain afternoons in the winter and summer seasons.

Golf. If golf is your game, don't miss the Doral-Ryder PGA Open at the Doral Hotel and Country Club or the Elizabeth Arden Classic held at Turnberry Isle in January or February.

Football. The Miami Dolphins, who are professional champions, play to capacity crowds in the Dolphin Sta-

Shopping

Miami is the sophisticated crossroads of the Caribbean, the place where all Latin America comes to shop.

If you're in the market for competitively priced electronic goods, gold jewellery and clothing, follow the crowds downtown to Flagler Street—or over to the Miami Free Zone (N.W. 107th Street). For ethnic items, explore the emporia of Calle Ocho in Little Havana, as well as the small shops in Coconut Grove, where merchants stock all kinds of pottery, handicraft and imports. And don't overlook Cauley Square, south of town on US 1. Collectibles and arts and crafts are the speciality in this village of wood-frame shops dating from the Flagler era.

Some of the best window shopping in town is along Decorator's Row (40th Street between N.E. 2nd Avenue and Miami Avenue). Showrooms here display furniture, fixtures and fittings garnered from across the nation and around the world. Certain establishments open their doors "to the trade only", but an air of confidence will generally carry you across the threshold.

dium in north Dade. Fans also turn out in the Orange Bowl for that winning varsity team, the University of Miami Hurricanes. Go for the experience, if not the game.

Baseball. Spring training brings the Baltimore Orioles to Miami Stadium (2301 N.W. 10th Avenue) in March and April. See them play teams based elsewhere in Florida in the "Grapefruit League" games, a prelude to the summer season.

Speedboat Racing. High-speed power boats churn up the foam at the bayfront Miami Marine Stadium, venue for races all year round.

For the most part, Miami's department and chain stores are concentrated in vast, air-conditioned malls like North Miami's Aventura, Omni International in Biscayne Boulevard and Dadeland (largest in the south-east), off US 1 in North Kendall Drive. The exclusive big stores (Neiman Marcus, Bonwit Teller, Saks Fifth Avenue, Lord and Taylor, Bloomingdale's) and designer boutiques have premises in the prestige malls of Bal Harbour, Mayfair-in-the-Grove and The Falls in South Dade—all distinguished by their inventive architecture, landscaping and display.

Check in the local papers for details of sales and special offers. Or shop in Fashion District outlets (N.W. 5th Avenue between 24th and 29th streets) for all-year-round bargains in designer clothing and accessories and Miami-manufactured articles. Certain retail chains carry nothing but discounted merchandise, notably Loehmann's (clothes) and Luria's (houseware and small electrical appliances).

Best Buys

Prices can vary considerably, so shop around before you put your money down.

86 **Active sportswear**. Ameri-can manufacturers lead the field when it comes to aerobic clothing and track suits, the uniform of the 80s. The fanciful golf and tennis gear is guaranteed to change your image, if not your game.

Children's clothing. Dress your child American-style in miniature track suits, sturdy overalls and denims.

Cigars. Hand-rolled Havanas made in Miami are the authentic Cuban article.

Citrus fruit. Send yourself a crate of Florida oranges or grapefruit. Miami fruit shippers (including several concerns at the airport) air-freight fruit all over the U.S. and around the world.

Cosmetics and toiletries. Sun preparations include a sophisticated range of tanning lotions and some esoteric blocking ointments and creams for complete protection from ultra-violet rays. Locally made beauty products incorporate rejuvenating papaya enzymes and the healing sap of the aloe plant.

Electronics. You can choose from an array of Japanese- and American-made cameras,

Looking for something a little bit different? Trendy shoppers make for the Grove.

The Palm Palm Co.

GIFTS CARDS
RESORTWEAR

computers, radios and other goods. The prices are as interesting as the competition is keen.

Foodstuffs. Carry home the taste of the tropics in the form of Florida coconut patties, chocolate-covered citrus peel and orange-blossom honey. Stock up on enough Cuban coffee to last until your next trip—vacuum-packed in tins and lightweight plastic packets.

Gadgets. You'll find a variety of handy implements, from serrated grapefruit knives to a special plastic straw that allows you to drink juice direct from the orange.

*From religious relics to radios—
you can buy it second-hand in
Little Havana.*

Indian handicraft. Miccosukee craftswomen fashion
traditional patchwork gar-
ments, beaded necklaces and
palmetto fibre dolls, all available at the village in Tamiami
Trail.

Jewellery. Look for adorn-
ments of shell, glass and semi-
precious stones—or the nar-
row gold bangle bracelets
Cuban women favour.

Linens. Designer collections
for the bed and bath combine
ease of care with original
styling.

Resort clothing. American
designers pioneered the casual
look and they still do it better
than anyone else. Be as traditional or as trendy as you like
in tropical whites, pastel linens and bright cottons. Some
of the most famous American
stylists produce inexpensive
lines with designer flair, including Halston, Calvin Klein
and others.

Shoes. Imports from Brazil,
Argentina and elsewhere in
South America are reasonably
priced.

Souvenirs. They run the
gamut from magnetic sea-
shells and driftwood lamp
stands to plastic alligators
—take your pick.

Swimwear. Miami lives at
the beach. The range of sizes
and styles is almost infinite.

Western gear. From hats,
boots and bandanas to silver-
studded belts, Miami outfitters supply both Dade County
dudes and urban cowboys. **89**

Entertainment

You can keep to the night-club circuit or concentrate on the cultural. Whatever your choice, there's plenty going on.

After dark, Miami moves to a Latin beat. People dress up and step out to supper clubs like Les Violins, Copacabana and the Flamenco, where Spanish guitars, Cuban show-girls and *folklórico* dancers share the spotlight in extravagant production numbers. And in between the shows, strolling violinists put lovers —Latin and others—into the appropriate mood. So have dinner and make a night of it, or take in one of the shows for the price of drinks and a cover charge.

Over on the Beach, the big hotels stage their own lavish floor shows featuring American-style chorus lines, known singers and comedy acts in season. If you don't feel like club-hopping on your own, join a bus tour and go around with a group.

There are lots of discos, some with live groups. Piano bars specialise in mood music,

drinks and, perhaps, dinner. The lively cocktail lounges have jazz combos, rock groups, soul or pop singers on hand. Romantic trios play in the lounges of the more elegant hotels, where sedate couples may be seen dancing cheek to cheek.

Greater Miami loves a show. Broadway hits come to Coconut Grove Playhouse, while the big Broadway musicals open at the Miami Beach Theater of the Performing

After dark, action gravitates to the Grove.

Arts. Less commercial off-Broadway fare is the province of the South of Broadway group, based downtown at the Knight Center. The South Florida Theater Company brings Shakespeare to the gardens of Vizcaya for two months of open-air performances every winter.

Teatro Avante, Teatro Bellas Artes and other Hispanic theatre groups stage both popular and experimental plays. You'll have a fascinating evening ahead of you, if your Spanish is up to it.

Concerts classical and popular take place at the Dade County Auditorium, Gusman Cultural Center and Theater of the Performing Arts on the Beach, as well as at local churches and temples. From October to May, internationally renowned performers and orchestras come to town for the Prestige, Great Artists and International Artists series. Throughout the year, the Per-

forming Arts for Community and Education authority (P.A.C.E.) organises excellent free events like the popular Big Orange Festival. There's also a season of opera, presented in English (national series) and the original language (international series) by the Greater Miami Opera.

The leading American modern dance companies make regular appearances here. You'll also have the chance to see fine local groups like Dance Miami and the Momentum Dance Company, which feature new work by Florida choreographers. In another vein, the Ballet Concerto Company perpetuates the traditions of the Cuban National Ballet.

Cinemas all over town show the popular Hollywood blockbusters, and art houses like the Arcadia, Beaumont and Cinematheque in the Gables and the Grove Cinema screen classic and avant-garde films from around the world in the original version. Little Havana specialises in Spanish-language diversions. Consult the schedules in the daily newspapers.

Supper clubs and floor shows—that's entertainment in Miami.

Calendar of Events

January
: *Three Kings' Parade*. Little Havana steps out on the Sunday nearest Epiphany (January 6).
: *Art Deco Weekend*. Vintage car rallies, jazz concerts and fancy dress balls recreate the mood of the Gatsby era, while exhibitions, lectures and tours put the period into perspective. On Miami Beach.

February
: *Big Orange Music Festival*. Classical performers and stars of rock, pop, jazz and reggae drop into Miami for a series of free concerts in the open air.
: *Miami Grand Prix*. Racing drivers from all over test their skill on the streets of downtown Miami.

February/March
: *Carnaval Miami*. Carnival in Miami means ten days of Latin-style festivities, climaxing in Calle Ocho Open House, a street party in Little Havana attended by close on a million people.

March
: *Italian Renaissance Festival*. Chainmail garment makers, bookbinders and madrigal singers do their thing at Vizcaya. Enjoy Italian food, music and dancing.

April
: *Salute to Canada Week*. The resort of Surfside fêtes holidaymakers from north of the border with a full programme of theatre, concerts and sporting events.

June
: *Bahamas Goombay Festival*. Descendants of Coconut Grove's original Bahamian settlers recall the food, music and crafts of their island of origin.

July
: *All American Celebration*. Miami Beach throws a big party on the Fourth of July—and everyone's invited. Free concerts are a highlight of the oceanside revels.

October
: *Baynanza*. Attention turns to Biscayne Bay for a week of events that include the Columbus Day regatta and fairs at Haulover Park and the Port of Miami.

November
: *Florida Renaissance Fayre*. See knights joust on Key Biscayne—or watch a play of the period.

December
: *Miccosukee Indian Arts Festival*. Music, dance and art are on the agenda when Indian tribes from throughout the Americas get together at the Miccosukee village.

December/January
: *Orange Bowl Festival*. Not one event but many. The festival culminates in the King Orange Jamboree Parade, a nationally televised nighttime extravaganza.

Eating Out

The possibilities have burgeoned with the population. You can sample Southern home cooking as authentic as any this side of the Mason-Dixon line and kosher fare to compare with New York's best. But the real gastronomic news in Miami is the explosion of interest in ethnic food—Cuban cuisine first and foremost, but also Mexican, Haitian, Greek, Indian, Japanese and Thai.

South Dade farmers supply chefs with a bounty of fresh fruit and vegetables, and offshore waters provide plenty of fish and shellfish. Everglades frog legs turn up on some menus and you may just come across alligator meat. It's farmed out in the glades, though consumption is, for the time being, limited.

Meal Times

Most restaurants serve breakfast from 7 to 11 a.m., and lunch from about 11.30 to 1.30 p.m. or so. Dinner is available from 5 or 6 p.m. until 10 or 11, with the exception of Little Havana establishments and a few others on the Beach, which don't close down till 12 or 1 in the morning—even later at weekends.

Some restaurants offer an "early bird special", a menu at a reduced price to diners who order their evening meal before 6 o'clock, or thereabouts. A brunch menu is widely available on Sundays from 11 a.m. to 3 p.m. If hunger strikes in the middle of the night, make for one of the chain coffee shops, open 24 hours.

Where to Eat

Miami's best restaurants are concentrated in the Gables, the Grove and the Beach. You can dine on the oceanfront, in sight of the sea, in Deco surroundings or a garden setting, around an open hearth. Gamble while you eat at the race track, dog track or jai-alai fronton. Or have a meal at one of the theme restaurants that evoke medieval Spain or Tudor England.

In the more elegant establishments, jacket or jacket and tie are required, but for the most part you can cultivate a casual appearance. A lot of oceanfront hotels ban improperly attired swimmers from indoor restaurants, so be

Work on your sun-tan while you eat. Terrace restaurants open for business all year round in subtropical Miami.

prepared with shoes and a cover-up.

Coffee shops serve sandwiches, salads, light meals and snacks—but no alcohol. If you're in a hurry, sit at the counter for faster service.

Delicatessens specialise in sandwiches, pastries and kosher dishes. Long queues form outside the popular delis at peak hours, but they generally move quickly. If you don't want to wait, put in your order "to go". There's usually a special window or queue for take-out service.

Fast food outlets include local ethnic franchises, usually to be found at the big shop-

ping centres. Order from the counter of your choice—Greek, Italian, Cuban, Japanese, whatever—and take a seat afterwards in the central courtyard.

Juice bars feature fruit and vegetable juices, including fresh-squeezed orange and grapefruit. Have a *piña colada*—pineapple juice and coconut milk, without the rum.

Health restaurants emphasize fruit and vegetable preparations, though some do serve fish. The produce used is often organically grown.

Cafeterias cater to people on a budget or in a hurry. You take a tray and choose your meal from a selection of hot and cold dishes. Items that are cooked to order will be brought to you when they're ready. At some cafeterias, you carry your tray to the table yourself. At others, a waiter performs this service, for which he expects a small tip. Usually you pay the cashier as you leave.

Eating Habits

For Europeans, certain American customs may be unfamiliar, if not downright bewildering. The predilection for ice in drinks, for example, causes consternation. Nothing escapes the cold treatment, from whisky to cola. If you prefer your drinks cool, but not iced, remember to say so when you order.

The coffee ritual (like the coffee itself) takes a bit of getting used to. The brew is weak by European standards—and the cup is "bottomless". That means the waiter will refill it repeatedly without extra charge.

Don't be surprised if your waiter urges you to take your leftovers home in a "doggie bag". Some restaurants serve far more than one person can eat on the assumption that customers will carry away what they don't consume on the spot. Even cafeterias supply doggie bags, but you have to wrap up the food yourself.

What to Eat

Breakfast. Start the day right at a deli with coffee and a Danish, a kind of sweet roll with a prune, cinnamon-and-nut, custard or cheese filling. If you can't make up your mind, order an assortment of mini-Danishes and try them all. Or opt for bagels (whole-wheat bagels for the health-conscious!) with butter or cream cheese and jam.

Cuban street counters provide a compelling alternative in the form of guava pastries hot from the oven *(pastelitos de guayaba)* or toasted Cuban bread. If you like your coffee strong, a Cuban breakfast is the only breakfast. Have an eye-opening *café cubano,* strong and black, or *café con leche,* coffee with milk and sugar. Be sure to specify "no sugar" if you prefer unsweetened coffee.

The American option—"eggs any style"—comes Southern-style with grits (a cornmeal gruel) or with traditional home fries (sliced, sautéed potatoes) or hash brown potatoes (grated and fried with onion).

Brunch. This hybrid of breakfast and lunch leans more towards the former, though alcohol is admissible, especially a morning pick-me-up like a Screwdriver or Bloody Mary. You can eat any breakfast food, though the classic dish is eggs Benedict—poached eggs and ham on English muffins (rather like a crumpet), topped with Hollandaise sauce. Seafood pancakes and chicken à la reine (in a cream sauce with mushrooms) are popular for brunch, too. A lot of Miami hotels feature a brunch buffet on Sundays.

Sandwiches. The deli variety includes corned beef, turkey, roast beef, smoked tongue and pastrami (a kind of cured beef) stacked on your choice of bread—white, wholewheat, rye, pumpernickel—or rolls. Lox (smoked salmon) and cream cheese are a popular Jewish combination, served on a bagel.

Pita or Arab flat bread may be filled with tuna (tunny), egg or chicken salads. A club sandwich is a layered collation of chicken, bacon, tomato and lettuce with mayonnaise on toast.

You'll have a job stretching your mouth around a Cuban sandwich—it's piled so high with sugar-cured ham, pork, Swiss cheese (an American original) and pickles. Leave it to the Cubans to improve on the hamburger: the *frita* adds minced pork to the beef, as well as garlic, paprika, vinegar and spices.

Soups. Green turtle soup, a clear broth made from the flippers, is typically Floridian, as are spicy chowders that contain conch (a kind of shellfish). Delis ladle out borscht by the bowlful. Try this beetroot soup hot, or cold with sour cream. Chicken soup is more than a food; it's the home remedy every Jewish mother prescribes for whatever ails you. Add a matzoh

Picnicking under the pines at Cape Florida, on Key Biscayne.

meal dumpling to the clear broth and you have nourishing matzoh ball soup.

Salads. The standard sort consists of shredded mixed greens or iceberg lettuce and sliced tomatoes with a choice of dressing: creamy, tomato-flavoured French, Russian (mayonnaise, tomato ketchup), Thousand Island (mayonnaise, chilli sauce, pickle relish), Italian (oil, vinegar, garlic, herbs) and Roquefort. Cole slaw is often served with hamburgers, sandwiches

itself. Chef's Salad combines ham, turkey, tongue, roast beef or other cold meats and sliced tomatoes on a bed of iceberg lettuce. Raw spinach salad is topped with sliced onion, mushrooms and hard-boiled egg. Popular with garlic lovers, Caesar salad blends crisp romaine lettuce and hard-boiled egg with croutons in a garlic-flavoured parmesan dressing.

Florida fruit salads are frequently—but not always—composed of fresh fruit. Depending on the season, you may be served a medley of mango, papaya, starfruit, grapefruit, orange, watermelon and canteloupe with your choice of frozen yogurt, sherbet (sorbet) or cottage cheese. Southerners are fond of ambrosia, sugared orange slices and grated fresh coconut.

Meat. Miami's steak houses and American-style establishments cater to the national passion for thick sirloin steaks and prime ribs. Open-hearth restaurants specialise in tangy barbecued ribs—usually baby beef—grilled over hot coals.

Old-world chicken in the pot (boiled chicken) and beef flanken (stew) are great kosher favourites. Creamed chicken and biscuits (soft rolls

or fried fish. Usually the shredded cabbage and carrot are mixed with mayonnaise, but a sweet vinaigrette dressing may also be used. Many restaurants feature a self-service salad bar, laden with greens and a variety of garnishes.

A salad can be a meal in

leavened with baking powder) and baked Virginia ham come straight from the old plantation.

Fish and Shellfish. Order the catch of the day—flaky white Florida snapper, grouper or sea trout grilled, fried or sautéed in butter. The more delicate pompano is often prepared *en papillote* (baked in paper), a procedure that enhances the subtle flavour. You can eat the delicious dolphin with impunity; it bears no relation to Flipper and his friends. New England scrod often appears on local menus. It's usually fresh, but it's not from Florida. Hush puppies (fried balls of cornmeal and onion) may accompany fried fish and shellfish.

At a deli, have gefilte fish, a mixture of whitefish, egg and matzoh meal, eaten cold or, occasionally, hot.

Some restaurants will cook your own catch of the day for you if you clean the fish first. The service charge usually includes all the trimmings.

Fresh jumbo shrimps (and not all shrimps are fresh, even in Florida) usually come from the Gulf. Cold shrimp dishes include shrimp cocktail with red sauce (chilli sauce and horse-radish), shrimp salad with mayonnaise dressing and shrimp Louis with hard-boiled egg and Russian dressing. Shrimps are good skewered and grilled, breaded and sautéed with garlic (in which case they're called scampi), or deep-fried with tartare sauce. If you're not counting calories, indulge in seafood newburg, a combination of shrimps, scallops and lobster in a rich, tomato-flavoured cream sauce.

Lobster in Miami may mean the Maine variety (with claws) or spiny lobster, also called crawfish or Florida lobster. The taste and texture of this warm-water crustacean are distinctive—and no less delectable to the initiated. Ask for it boiled with lemon and butter sauce and savour the nut-like flavour to the full.

Oysters and clams are served raw on the half shell, baked or fried. But the big treat is Florida stone crabs, in season from October 15 to April 15. You eat only the claws—one is taken from the crab, which is returned to the water to grow another—hot with lemon and butter or cold with mustard mayonnaise. Most restaurants crack the shell well with a wooden mallet before serving, so you probably won't need the battery of implements you'll be given to extract the sweet meat. All the same, it can be a messy business, so don't be surprised if your waiter produces a big paper bib and ties it round you toddler fashion.

Most restaurants that serve seafood propose a cold seafood platter with a selection of stone crab, shrimps, clams, oysters and Florida lobster—or a fried Fisherman's Platter, including shrimps, oysters, scallops, clams and fish fingers.

Vegetables. Satisfy a craving for the fresh variety at health restaurants, where mixed vegetables are lightly steamed or stir-fried. Southern cooks have a way of their own with vegetables. Try stewed tomatoes (cooked with bread and a pinch of sugar), fried eggplant (aubergine), creamed onions and candied yams (sweet potatoes glazed with sugar).

Desserts. Creamy, calorific Key lime pie is a south Florida original. The real thing contains the fresh juice of Key limes and, like the fruit, is yellow, not green. A meringue topping is traditional. Southern pecan pie plays havoc with the waistline, too. The pecans are folded into a sweet mixture of corn syrup and egg yolk that's cloying to some, divine to others. Cheesecake reigns supreme among deli delights. And American apple pie is no stranger to Miami. Go all the way and have it "à la mode", with a scoop of rich vanilla ice cream.

Cuban food. Little Havana is the place to experiment. While you're mulling over the menu, order a drink—some sangría, perhaps—with *tostones* (fried slices of green plantain chips), *boniatos mariquitas* (fried slices of sweet potato) and *malanguitas* (similar to potato crisps)—all usually made to order.

For starters, plump for *sopón marinero* (shellfish soup with rice, peas and red pepper) or the more traditional black bean soup *(sopa de frijoles negros)*, flavoured with olive oil, garlic, salt pork and vinegar. Alternatives include *empanadas*, baked or fried meat pies filled with ham, chicken, pork or sausage, and chicken, beef or fish croquettes.

Cuban rice dishes are famous: *arroz con pollo*, chicken and saffran rice, and *arroz con camarones*, shrimps and saffron rice. *Piccadillo*—highly seasoned minced meat with red or green peppers, onion, tomatoes and garlic—is a simple dish that can be very good if it's freshly made.

Try Florida papaya, orange or grapefruit juice—it's only natural.

Chopped onion and wedges of lime always accompany grilled meats: *bistec de cerdo* (pork) or *hígado* (liver) and thinly sliced *palomilla,* the king of Cuban steaks. For real sustenance, choose *boliche mechado,* a kind of stew, or *carne asada,* roast meat in a sauce with potatoes.

The most popular accom- paniments are fried ripe plan- tains *(plátanos fritos),* and white rice, or rice and black beans cooked together, a sta- ple known as *moros* or *arroz moros. Yuca* and *malanga* are to Cubans what potatoes are to Anglos. The taste is fairly bland—until you add a gener- ous dollop of *mojito criollo,* a piquant sauce made of sour orange juice, olive oil and garlic.

Like your fellow diners, you may find it hard to resist dessert, be it *flan* (caramel custard), *tocino del cielo,* a very rich, very sweet confection made of sugar and egg yolks, or *buñuelos,* deep-fried pastries covered in syrup. The Cubans of Miami are also partial to a Nicaragua sweet known as *tres leches,* sponge cake saturated in the "three milks" of the title—whole, evaporated and condensed.

Afterwards, a cup of strong Cuban coffee will set you up for the rest of the day, or night, as the case may be.

Creole cooking. Restaurants in Little Haiti offer all the typical dishes, beginning with *griot*. Haitians can't get enough of this snack food, made of pork that's first boiled, then fried in its own fat. Spicy Creole stews may incorporate goat or conch, the latter known to the Haitians as *lambi*. To go with it, there's boiled corn meal, rice and beans and fried plantains.

A speciality of neighbourhood juice bars, Haitian fruit sodas (syrup and seltzer water) include some exotic varieties, and there's no end to the different kinds of fresh, tropical fruit juices.

Drinks

People in Miami often order iced tea with their meals, and wine is growing in popularity. New York state produces some good wines, but those from California are better. You can order domestic wine by the bottle, carafe or glass. Cuban restaurants feature Spanish wines, sangría and cider. You'll find American beer blander and more highly carbonated than the European variety—and it's served ice-cold. Imported beers are widely available.

Some people drink cocktails with their food in lieu of wine. Others indulge during the late-afternoon "happy hour", when bars serve free snacks with drinks, or two drinks for the price of one. Southern tipplers like Kentucky bourbon, a mellow whisky distilled from corn, malt and rye. You drink it neat, on the rocks or with soda. From the old Havana to the new Miami comes the *Cuba libre,* a combination of rum, lime juice and cola. Another rum drink, the daiquiri, contains lemon juice and sugar. Beware of the all-American dry martini. This blend of gin and dry vermouth packs a considerable punch.

Bottoms up!

BLUEPRINT for a Perfect Trip

How to Get There

Although the fares and conditions described below have all been carefully checked, it is advisable to consult a travel agent for the latest information on fares and other arrangements.

From North America

BY AIR: Greater Miami is easily accessible from the larger northern, midwestern and western cities. There are many non-stop flights every day to Miami from New York, Chicago, Los Angeles and San Francisco.

BY BUS: Miami is served by Greyhound/Trailways, Inc. coach.

BY RAIL: Amtrak is currently advertising a variety of bargain fares, including Excursion and Family fares and tour packages with hotel and guide included.

BY CAR: Travellers coming down the east coast can take Interstate 95 via Washington and Savannah. The toll turnpike system, another possibility, links up with the Sunshine State Parkway. The shortest route from the west coast is Interstate 10, passing Tucson, El Paso, Houston and Mobile.

From Great Britain

BY AIR: There are daily non-stop flights from Heathrow and Gatwick to Miami. Some U.S. airlines offer travellers from abroad a discount on the cost of each internal flight, or flat-rate unlimited-travel tickets for specific periods.

Charter Flights and Package Tours: Advance Booking Charter (ABC) flights depart from London Gatwick for Miami. Many package tours are available, including camper holidays, coach tours, excursions to the Bahamas, trips to other American cities and sights, etc. Many Caribbean cruises originate in Miami, "cruise capital of the world".

Baggage. Baggage allowances for scheduled transatlantic flights are complex, but you are allowed to check in, free, two suitcases of normal size. In addition, one piece of hand baggage of a size which fits easily under the aircraft seat may be carried on board. Confirm size and weight restrictions with your travel agent or air carrier when booking your ticket.

It is advisable to insure all luggage for the duration of your trip. Any travel agent can make the necessary arrangements.

When to Go

Winter is the tourist season in sub-tropical South Florida. Days are warm and sunny and nights, pleasantly cool. Some years, the occasional cold spell can send temperatures plummeting to near freezing point for a day or two, but that's the exception, not the rule.

Most of the rainfall for the year occurs in summer, in late afternoon showers that cool the air and leave mornings and early afternoons free for beaching and sunbathing. Summers in Miami may be hot and humid, but thanks to the trade winds they're rarely unbearable—and air-conditioning systems do double duty.

Average daytime temperatures:

		J	F	M	A	M	J	J	A	S	O	N	D
Maximum	°F	74	75	78	80	84	86	88	88	87	83	78	76
	°C	23	24	26	27	29	30	31	31	31	28	26	24
Minimum	°F	61	61	64	67	71	74	76	76	75	72	66	62
	°C	16	16	18	19	22	23	24	24	24	22	19	17

* Minimum temperatures are measured just before sunrise, maximum temperatures in the afternoon.

Planning Your Budget

To give you an idea of what to expect, here's a list of prices in U.S. dollars. They can only be regarded as approximate, however, as inflation pushes the cost of living ever higher.

Airport transfer. Airport Region Taxi Service Zone A $4.50, Zone B $7. Red Top Sedan Service $6.75–10.25, depending on destination. Taxi to central Coral Gables $8, to downtown Miami $11, to Port of Miami $12, to Miami Beach up to $25.

Attractions. Seaquarium $13.95 adults, $9.95 children up to 12; Parrot Jungle $8.50 adults, $4 children 6–12; Fairchild Tropical Garden $4 adults, children 12 and under free; Vizcaya $6 adults, children under 6 free, students $5; The Barnacle $1.

Babysitter. $4–5 per hour for one or two children, $1 for each additional child, plus transport expenses. Hotels charge $6–8 per hour.

Bicycle hire. $3 per hour, $15 per day, $35 per week (three speed).

Camping. From $6 per day, per site.

Car hire. Rates vary considerably with the company and the season. By way of comparison, here is the price of a Chevrolet Cavalier with 100 free miles during the high season: $158 per week, $36 per day.

Cigarettes (20). $1.75; higher for foreign brands.

Entertainment. Cinema $5–7; nightclub/discotheque $5–20 cover charges, $4–6 drinks.

Hairdressers. Man's haircut $7–25; Woman's haircut $25, cut, shampoo and set $15–30, colour rinse/dye $10–50.

Hotels. Double room with bath: de luxe from $120, moderate $70–90, budget $40–60.

Meals and drinks. Continental breakfast $2–3, full breakfast $4–7, lunch in snack bar $5, in restaurant $7.50–14, dinner $15–30 (more with entertainment), coffee $1, espresso $1.50–2, beer $2.50–3, glass of wine $2.50–3, carafe $6–7, bottle from $10, cocktail $3.50–5.

Metrobus. Local $1, express $1.25, students and seniors 50¢, transfer 25¢.

Metrorail. $1, students and seniors 50¢. Pass (one month) $50.

Taxis. $1, plus $1.20 per mile.

Metromover. 25¢.

An A–Z Summary of Practical Information and Facts

A   **ACCOMMODATION** (See also Camping). Book a room downtown, on the beach or in one of Miami's palmy suburbs. Whatever your budget, there's a wide variety of accommodation to choose from. Reservations for hotels and motels in Greater Miami can be made from 8 a.m. to 8 p.m. daily by dialling the Greater Miami Reservation System; tel. 866-0366 or 1-800-356-8392 (U.S.) or 1-800-248-3380 (Canada).

Bear in mind that rooms are at a premium during the peak tourist season (December 15 to Easter), above all at Christmastime and during the Easter holiday period. Summer can be busy, too, and rooms may be hard to come by during the Fourth of July and Labor Day weekends.

On the oceanfront, rooms with a sea view are always more expensive. Private bath, colour television and air conditioning are standard. Most of the larger hotels employ a hall porter, referred to in the United States as a "bell captain".

Many hotel and motel chains make no charge for children under 18 sharing a room with their parents. Inquire about "family plans" when you book. Some establishments offer special rates to guests who take their meals on the premises: A.P. (American Plan) includes three meals a day and M.A.P. (Modified American Plan), breakfast and lunch or dinner.

Certain luxury hotels have suites only—bedroom and sitting room with kitchenette. In some areas you'll see signs advertising "efficiencies" or "pullmanettes"—modest bed-sitting rooms with cooking facilities. A minimum stay may be required.

A resort tax of 5% is added to hotel and motel bills in Greater Miami (less in the communities of Bal Harbour and Surfside). Florida has an additional 6% sales tax.

Most hotels request that guests leave their rooms by noon on the day of departure. Check-in time is usually 3 p.m.

Airport hotels. The Miami International Airport Hotel has its premises in the main terminal building, on Concourse E. A score of hotels situated on the perimeter of the airfield provide free mini-bus transport to and from the terminal.

Art Deco hotels. A group of renovated oceanfront hotels from the Jazz Age attract a trendy young crowd to the Art Deco National Historic

District on the south shore of Miami Beach. Smaller and more personal than the newer beach resorts, these hotels feature 1930s-era atmosphere in sight of the sea. To make a reservation, contact Art Deco Hotels:

1236 Ocean Drive, P.O. Box 19000-E, Miami Beach, FL 33139-2030; tel. 534-2135.

Youth accommodation. The Greater Miami area has one youth hostel, the Clay Hotel, 1438 Washington Avenue, Miami Beach, FL 33139; tel. (305) 534-2988.

AIRPORT. Conveniently situated just west of the city centre, Miami International Airport is about 15 minutes by car from the downtown district, and 25 minutes from Miami Beach. Served by more airlines than any other airport in the United States, Miami International is one of the world's busiest facilities.

The main terminal comprises two levels, divided into various concourses or zones, with domestic arrivals below and departures above. Currency exchange, a 24-hour information desk (Concourse E), telephones, luggage lockers, duty-free shops and numerous others are to be found on the upper level, along with various bars, fast-food restaurants, snack bars, and newsstands. Baggage-claim areas (show your ticket stubs to the security guard on the way out) and car hire agencies occupy the lower level.

An elevated "people mover" links the main terminal building to a satellite terminal for international flights. There are telephones, a restaurant, duty-free shops and newsstand. Processing is fast and courteous in the adjoining Customs and Immigration facility, where red and green channels are in operation.

Check-in procedure. Depending on your destination and airline, you may be able to check in for your flight and register your luggage at the kerbside. Arrive 45 minutes before domestic flights, one hour before international departures.

Ground transport. There are always plenty of taxis on hand for the trip into town. The bright blue vehicles of the Airport Region Taxi Service (ARTS) carry passengers to nearby destinations for a low flat fare. Red Top Sedan Service mini-buses provide transport to hotels downtown and on the Beach for about a third of the price of a taxi. Cheaper—but less convenient—are the municipal buses, leaving every 30 to 60 minutes from a stop outside the main terminal building. Ask at the information desk for route maps and details of connections.

B **BICYCLE HIRE**. Miami may well be the best place in the world to cycle. There are 138 miles of paved paths to explore, including highly scenic routes in Coral Gables, Key Biscayne and Coconut Grove. To hire a bike in the area of your choice, look in the *Yellow Pages* under "Bicycles–Renting". In addition to standard, three- and ten-speed models, tandem bikes are often available. Bicycles may be hired by the hour, day, week or month. You may have to pay a deposit or leave your driving licence or passport as a surety.

Out in Everglades National Park (Tamiami entrance), you can cycle along the 15-mile Shark Valley loop road, sighting rare birds and wild-life as you go. Standard bikes may be hired by the hour at the entrance gate.

C **CAMPING**. Camp sites are few and far between in urban Miami. Florida Kampgrounds (KOA) maintains two commercial sites in the greater metropolitan area—one on the southern outskirts of the city, the other to the north. A playground, games room, heated pool and jacuzzi are the pride of Miami North KOA, while a heated pool and hot tub bring campers 22 miles out to Miami South KOA, between Route 997 and US 1.

Miami North KOA, 14075 Biscayne Boulevard, North Miami Beach, FL 33181; tel. 940–4141.
Miami South KOA, 20675 S.W. 162nd Avenue, Miami, FL 33187; tel. 233-5300.

The Dade County Parks and Recreation Department administers the Larry and Penny Thompson Campground, a 240-acre pinewood preserve near Metrozoo. Tent sites and hook-ups for 240 caravans or recreational vehicles are available on a first come, first served basis.

Larry and Penny Thompson Campground, 12451 S.W. 184th Street, Miami, FL 33177; tel. 232-1049.

M.E. Thompson Park, 170th Street and NW 157th Avenue, Miami, FL; tel. 821-5122.

Designed for the handicapped, Bird Drive Park and Therapeutic Campground features a Vita course for wheelchair-bound athletes and a swimming pool with a hydraulic lift, as well as a nature trail with hand rails for the blind.

Bird Drive Park and Therapeutic Campground, 9401 S.W. 72nd Avenue, Miami, FL; tel. 665-5319.

There are various camping possibilities in the wilds of Dade County—but don't expect to commute to town. Farmland surrounds Southern

Comfort Campground, near the Florida City entrance to Everglades National Park. In the park itself, camping is permitted at Long Pine Key and Flamingo. Areas for camping have also been set aside in Biscayne National Park and Chekika State Recreation Area. It's a good idea to reserve in advance. Maximum stay is two weeks. Mosquitoes are a nuisance in summer. Take repellent.

Southern Comfort Campground, 345 E. Palm Drive, Florida City, FL 33034; tel. 248-6909.

Everglades National Park, P.O. Box 279, Homestead, FL 33030; tel. 247-6211.

Biscayne National Park, P.O. Box 1369, Homestead, FL 33090-1369; tel. 247-PARK.

Chekika State Recreation Area, S.W. 237th Avenue and Grossman Drive, Homestead, FL 33030; tel. 252-4438.

Camping at the roadside, in a car park or on private land without permission is both illegal and unsafe.

CAR HIRE. Competition for custom is lively, making rates in Miami among the lowest in the United States, even during the peak tourist period. It pays to shop around before you hire a car. As you compare the prices of the larger national firms with those of the numerous local companies, be sure to ascertain whether or not insurance cover is included. Rates fluctuate seasonally. Air conditioning is a standard feature.

To hire a car, you must be at least 21 years old and in possession of a valid driving licence. Some agencies make exceptions for 18-year-old drivers paying with their own credit cards. For tourists from non-English-speaking countries, a translation of the driving licence is highly recommended, together with the national licence itself, or failing this, an International Driving Permit.

You'll find it more convenient to settle your bill with a credit card, rather than cash. If you have no card, you must leave a sizable cash deposit—and cash might not be accepted at night or on weekends.

CHILDREN. The family-oriented resort hotels organize supervised activities for children of all ages.

Staff of the Children's Workshop in the Omni shopping centre mind infants and keep children of all ages entertained while their parents browse or sightsee. There's a two-hour minimum charge. For information, contact Children's Workshop International:

1601 Biscayne Boulevard, Miami, FL 33132; tel. 358-6500. **111**

C **CIGARETTES, CIGARS, TOBACCO**. Packets of cigarettes may vary in price by as much as one third, depending on where you buy them. A packet from a vending machine always costs more than one obtained in a supermarket or at a newsstand. The choice of pipe tobacco, both home-grown and imported, is vast. Cuban artisans still roll cigars by hand in Little Havana.

Clearly marked signs prohibiting smoking are visible in a number of public places. In restaurants there are often smoking and no-smoking sections.

CLIMATE and CLOTHING. Greater Miami delivers all the winter sun and warm weather a tourist could wish for. Daytime temperatures generally hover in the upper 70s Fahrenheit, although they can soar higher—or dip lower. So be prepared for every eventuality with an assortment of lightweight and heavier clothing. You can shop locally for whatever you need in the way of sportswear, from flamboyant golf and tennis gear to the world's widest selection of swimming costumes.

Miami swelters in summer, but you probably won't mind the heat. Air-conditioning systems work overtime, blowing arctic air everywhere—in restaurants, office buildings, enclosed shopping malls, on Metrobuses, Metrorail and Metromover, the automated "people mover". Always carry a wrap for the chilly indoors.

Day and night, winter and summer, casual resort clothing is appropriate in Miami. Men needn't wear a tie or even a jacket, except to dine out at better restaurants in the evening. Older Latin men show a preference for the *guayabera*, the shirt-cum-jacket of the tropics, made to measure by Cuban tailors in Little Havana.

As for footwear, sandals may be worn all year round in South Florida, but you'll need a pair of sturdy closed shoes for nature walks and excursions to the Everglades. Don't forget to bring your sunglasses; they're a must in Miami, where the glare of high noon can be blinding. Other indispensables include sun visors or hats, and rubber sandals for the beach.

COMMUNICATIONS (see also HOURS).

Post offices. The U.S. postal service deals only with mail. Telephone and telegraph services are operated by other companies. The main post office for Greater Miami lies west of the airport at

2200 Milam Dairy Road, Miami, FL 33152.

You can purchase stamps from machines in post office entrance halls
112 after closing time. Service is available after hours at the Miami

International Airport facility, alongside the main terminal building.
Post boxes are painted blue.

Poste restante (general delivery). You can have mail marked "General
Delivery" sent to you care of the main post office. Letters will be held for
up to a month. American Express offices also keep post for 30 days;
envelopes should be marked "Client's Mail".

Take your driving licence or passport with you for identification.

Telegrams. American telegraph companies are run privately. They offer
domestic and overseas services, as well as domestic telex facilities, and
are listed in the *Yellow Pages*. You can telephone the telegraph office,
dictate the message and have the charge added to your hotel bill, or
dictate it from a coin-operated phone and pay on the spot. A letter
telegram (night letter) costs about half the standard rate.

Telephone. The independent American telephone systems are efficient
and reliable. Phone boxes are found in the streets, at many service
stations, in shopping plazas, in restaurants and in most public buildings.

To make a local call, lift the receiver, put 25¢ in the appropriate slot,
wait for the dialling tone, then dial the seven-digit number. For local
information, ring 411. For local operator assistance, and for help within
the same area code, dial "0".

Long-distance and many international calls may be dialled direct,
even from a pay phone, if you follow the posted directions. If you don't
know the correct area code, dial "00" for operator assistance. Long-
distance calls cost more from a pay phone than from a private one.

Telephone rates are listed in the white pages of the telephone
directory. Also included is information on personal, reverse-charge and
credit card calls. All numbers with an 800 prefix are toll-free. Cheapest
calls can be made from a private phone at night, during weekends and on
public holidays—when rates drop considerably.

COMPLAINTS. If you have a serious complaint about business
practices in the Miami area and have talked to no avail with the
manager of the establishment in question, contact the Consumer
Protection Division of Dade County,

140 W. Flagler Street, Miami, FL; tel. 375-4222,

or the Agriculture Department, Consumer Services Division,

The Capitol, Tallahassee, FL 32301; tel. 1-800-342-2176.

The head office serves as a clearing house for complaints and will refer
callers to a Dade County number if necessary.

C **CONSULATES.** Few English-speaking countries maintain a consulate in Florida.

Australia: 636 5th Avenue, New York; tel. (212) 245-4000.

Canada: 1251 Avenue of the Americas, New York; tel. (212) 586-2400.

Eire: 515 Madison Avenue, New York; tel. (212) 319-2555.

New Zealand: Suite 530, 630 5th Avenue, New York; tel. (212) 586-0060.

South Africa: 425 Park Avenue, New York: tel. (212) 838-1700.

United Kingdom: 225 Peachtree Street N.E., Atlanta, Georgia; tel. (404) 524-5856.

CRIME and THEFT. Visitors would be wise to take the same precautions here as they would in any other big city. Store valuables and reserves of cash in the hotel safe, carrying only enough with you for your daily needs. Beware of pickpockets, many of whom work in pairs. They frequent city buses, queues, crowded stores and lifts.

To be on the safe side, go out after dark in groups, rather than alone, and leave your car with the attendant at a restaurant, night club or discotheque, instead of parking it yourself on a dimly-lit side street.

If a tourist avoids certain areas, especially those west and north-west of downtown, and follows the normal common-sense rules of behaviour, he need not be apprehensive.

CUSTOMS and ENTRY REGULATIONS. Canadians need only proof of nationality to enter the United States. Other foreign visitors require a visa, obtainable at U.S. embassies and consulates abroad. The application process can prove slow and difficult, depending on individual circumstances. When you apply, take along documents verifying your intention to return home.

A non-resident may claim, free of duty and taxes, articles up to $100 in value intended as gifts for other people. The exemption is valid only if the gifts accompany you, provided you stay 72 hours or more and if you have not claimed the exemption during the preceding 6 months. A hundred cigars may be included within this gift exemption.

Plants and foodstuffs also are subject to strict control; visitors from abroad may not import fruit, vegetables or meat. The same goes for chocolates that contain liqueur.

Passengers arriving or departing should declare any money or cheques exceeding $10,000.

Duty-free allowance. You will be asked to fill out a customs declaration form before you arrive in the U.S. The following chart shows what main duty-free items you may take into the U.S. (if you are over 21) and, when returning home, into your own country: **C**

Into:	Cigarettes	Cigars	Tobacco	Spirits	Wine
U.S.	200 or	50 or	2 kg.	1 l. or	1 l.
Australia	200 or	250 g. or	250 g.	1 l. or	1 l.
Canada	200 and	50 and	900 g.	1.1 l. or	1.1 l.
Eire	200 or	50 or	250 g.	1 l. and	2 l.
New Zealand	200 or	50 or	½ lb.	1 qt. and	1 qt.
South Africa	400 and	50 and	250 g.	1 l. and	2 l.
U.K.	200 or	50 or	250 g.	1 l. and	2 l.

DRIVING IN MIAMI. Drive on the right, overtake (pass) on the left. **D** The speed limit is 15 mph in school zones, 30 mph in business or residential districts, 55 mph on motorways (highways), unless otherwise indicated. If you keep within the flow of traffic, you'll have no problem, but if you go any faster a patrol car will pull you up.

There are various types of motorway in Greater Miami: turnpikes are high-speed dual carriageways that collect tolls; expressways and inter-state highways are usually free. Most maps indicate which roads collect tolls. It's a good idea to have a stock of coins on hand, as the "exact change" lanes move faster.

Try to avoid expressways and main thoroughfares during rush hours (7 to 9 a.m. and 4 to 6 p.m.), when traffic is reduced to a crawl.

Breakdowns. If you break down on a turnpike or expressway, pull over on to the righthand shoulder, lift up the bonnet and wait in the car (with doors locked!) for assistance. At night, use the hazard warning light. If your car is overheating, turn off the air conditioner—it's a strain on the engine.

Petrol (Gas) and Services. Many service stations have two "islands" —one for full service, the other for self service. You'll save money if you fill the tank yourself. The majority of stations close in the evenings and on Sundays.

D

Parking. Suburban malls and major tourist attractions provide ample free parking. At luxury malls, parking is cheaper with a "validated" ticket: any shopkeeper will stamp your ticket for you, even if you don't make a purchase. Many municipal car parks have meters; coins required and length of stay authorised are always indicated. In the city of Miami, parking can be difficult and expensive. If you plan to spend the day downtown, park your car at one of the outlying Metrorail stations and go into town by public transport. Be sure to park your car with, and not against, the flow of traffic. Do not park by a fire hydrant or alongside a kerb painted yellow.

Rules of the Road. Florida state law requires motorists in both directions to come to a complete halt when a school bus stops to pick up or drop off children. Throughout Dade County, you may turn right when the traffic lights are red if there are no pedestrians on the crossing—and no signs to the contrary. Be sure to come to a complete stop first. Otherwise, international rules of the road apply.

American Automobile Association. The AAA offers assistance to members of affiliated organisations abroad. It also provides travel information for South Florida and can arrange car insurance by the month for owner-drivers. Contact Greater Miami AAA East Florida: 4300 Biscayne Boulevard, Miami, FL 33137; tel. 573-5611.

Road signs. Although the United States has begun to change over to international pictographs, progress has been gradual and some differences remain between international and U.S. signs. The following list shows some of the different British and American terms.

American	*British*
Detour	Deviation
Divided highway	Dual carriageway
Expressway	Motorway
Men working	Roadworks
No passing	No overtaking
No parking along highway	Clearway
Railroad crossing	Level crossing
Traffic circle	Roundabout
Yield	Give way

DRUGS. Buying and selling hard drugs is a serious offence. Florida has a large force of undercover policemen who are battling to keep drugs out of the U.S.

ELECTRIC CURRENT. The U.S. has 110/115-volt 60-cycle A.C. Plugs are small, flat and two-pin; foreigners will need an adapter for razors and other appliances.

E

EMERGENCIES. Dial 911 to summon the police, an ambulance or the fire department.

The Emergency Room of Jackson Memorial Hospital at 1611 N.W. 12th Avenue in Miami will treat anyone in need of immediate attention.

GUIDES and TOURS. The services of a tour guide are provided for the price of admission to various historic sites, including Cape Florida Lighthouse, Vizcaya, The Barnacle and Coral Gables House. The Museum of Science employs "explainers"—university students who escort visitors around the exhibits on request. Fairchild Tropical Garden operates hourly guided tram tours for an additional charge; walking tours, scheduled several times daily, are free.

G

Several different companies operate bus and boat tours to sights and attractions in Greater Miami. Helicopter tours are also available. Ask your hotel or any travel agency for information, or consult *Destination Miami,* published by the Greater Miami Convention and Visitors Bureau.

The Miami Beach Design Preservation league offers tours of the Art Deco District on Saturdays at 10.30 a.m. For details, phone 672-2014.

In the national parks, rangers organise free nature walks, canoe trips and the like. Inquire at the visitors' centres for details. Concessionaires also run tram tours of Shark Valley and boat trips from Flamingo in Everglades National Park.

Officially sponsored boat excursions to Elliot Key are available from Convoy Point in Biscayne National Park. You travel aboard *Reef Rover III,* with an environmentalist and marine resources consultant, Capt. Ed Davison, at the helm. Or cruise the bay on the glass-bottom *Reef Rover IV.* To make reservations, call

Biscayne Aqua-Center, Inc., P.O. Box 1270, Homestead, FL 33030; tel. 247-2400.

HEALTH and MEDICAL CARE (see also EMERGENCIES). Foreign visitors should note that the United States doesn't provide free medical services and medical treatment is expensive. Arrangements should

H

H therefore be made in advance for temporary health insurance (through a travel agent or an insurance company).

If you arrive in Miami after flying through several time zones, take it easy for the first couple of days. Doctors recommend eating lightly initially, and getting plenty of rest.

Beware of the Florida sun. Use a sun screen or complete-block cream at first, and build up a tan gradually, in small doses. Far too many tourists overdo it, ruining their holiday. Remember that second- and third-degree burns can result from over-exposure. Be sure to protect your eyes as well. The sun's ultra-violet rays can irritate the delicate tissues of the cornea, especially when reflected off the surface of the sea or pool.

Visitors from Britain will find that certain drugs sold over the counter at home can be purchased only on prescription in the U.S. There's no shortage of drug stores, or pharmacies, but only a few of them stay open late at night.

HITCH-HIKING. The FBI and police advise strongly against accepting rides from strangers, and it is illegal on all highways.

HOURS. Offices in Greater Miami open from 9 a.m. to 5 p.m. Monday to Friday, and banks from 9 a.m. until 2 p.m. (later at the airport).

Post offices open from 8.30 a.m. to 5 p.m. Monday to Friday, till noon only on Saturdays. The airport facility provides service until 9 p.m. from Monday to Friday, till 12.30 p.m. on Saturdays.

Shops and department stores in central Miami and most other municipalities do business from 9 or 10 a.m. to 5.30 or 6 p.m., Monday to Saturday. However, most of the luxury malls and suburban shopping centres have extended hours, operating daily from 10 a.m. until 9 or 9.30 p.m. and from noon to 5 or 6.30 on Sundays. There are exceptions to this general rule. Certain centres may close several nights a week and others may open Sunday mornings, so it's a good idea to telephone before you make a special trip.

Restaurants generally serve lunch from 11 a.m. to 1.30 p.m., dinner from 5 p.m. to 10 or 11 p.m. (even midnight and after at a few places, especially on Calle Ocho). Fast-food outlets open from 6.30 a.m. (7.30 Sundays) to midnight or 1 a.m. A few coffee shops provide round-the-clock service.

Most tourist attractions open their doors seven days a week from 9 or 10 a.m. to 5 or 6 p.m. The ticket windows at the Seaquarium, Planet **118** Ocean and Metrozoo shut 1½ hours before closing time.

LANGUAGE. Spanish runs a close second to English in Miami, with its burgeoning Hispanic community. In some parts of the city, especially downtown, Little Havana and Hialeah, you may be addressed in Spanish first and then English, particularly by members of the older generation or by new arrivals from south of the border. For a time, Miami declared itself a bilingual city, but the emphasis nowadays is on English.

You'll hear some Yiddish spoken in the southern reaches of Miami Beach, home to a fair number of Jewish-Americans of Eastern European origin, while Creole holds sway in Little Haiti—making Miami a truly cosmopolitan city.

Some English-speaking foreigners are no less bewildered by certain American words and phrases. The following are a few that can be a source of confusion:

U.S.	British	U.S.	British
admission	entry fee	pavement	road surface
bathroom	toilet (private)	purse/	
bill	note (money)	pocketbook	handbag
billfold	wallet	rest room	toilet
check	bill (restaurant)	round-trip	return (ticket)
collect call	reverse-charge call	second floor	first floor
		sidewalk	pavement
dead end	cul-de-sac	stand in line	queue up
elevator	lift	trailer	caravan
first floor	ground floor	underpass	subway
gasoline	petrol	vest	waistcoat
liquor	spirits	wash up	wash oneself
liquor store	off-licence	windshield	windscreen
minister	clergyman	yard	garden

LOST PROPERTY. If you lose something in a public building, chances are it will be turned in to the "lost and found department". Restaurants and taxi companies hold lost articles in the hope that someone will retrieve them. Should you leave something behind on public transport, be it bus or rail, call 375-3366. Otherwise, contact the police department in the municipality where the loss occurred. Report the loss of your passport to the nearest consulate as well (see p. 114).

MAPS. Miami is changing so quickly, it's essential to procure a current town plan. Available in book shops, the Rand McNally map of Miami

M and Miami Beach takes in all 27 of the Greater Miami municipalities. The South Florida Map Company publishes an excellent plan of Miami and Metropolitan Dade County, including individual maps of Miami and Coral Gables. The Chamber of Commerce in each municipality distributes free maps, as does the Greater Miami Convention & Visitors Bureau.

Any marine suppliers and most book shops carry up-to-date navigation charts prepared by the National Ocean Survey. Chart 11467 gives full details of offshore waters from Elliott Key north to Lake Worth.

The maps in this guide were prepared by Falk-Verlag, Hamburg.

MEETING PEOPLE. Like most Americans, the people of Miami are friendly, open and easy to meet. Miamians will quickly spot a foreigner and start to chat, inquiring about your accent, where you're from, where you're staying, how you like their city. Perhaps the best place to make new friends is around the hotel pool, but you'll find yourself coming into contact with people almost everywhere—waiting in a queue, visiting a museum, shopping for a swimming costume.

MONEY MATTERS

Currency. The dollar is divided into 100 cents.

Bank notes: $1, $2 (rare), $5, $10, $20, $50 and $100. Larger denominations are not in general circulation. All notes are the same shape and colour, so it's easy to confuse them. Try to separate large and small denominations.

Coins: 1¢ (called a "penny"), 5¢ ("nickel"), 10¢ ("dime"), 25¢ ("quarter"), 50¢ ("half dollar") and $1. You may inadvertently be given Canadian or other foreign coins in change. Canadian coins are worth about 15% less than U.S. ones, and they do not work in automatic machines, such as telephones.

Banks and currency exchange (see also HOURS). Very few branch banks change foreign currency. Unless you are planning to go downtown, Miami International Airport is probably the most convenient place to make transactions. Some hotels change money, but the rate is not advantageous. It is simpler to carry dollar traveller's cheques (see below) or major credit cards.

When changing money or traveller's cheques, ask for $20 notes, which are accepted everywhere; some establishments refuse larger notes unless **120** they nearly equal the amount to be paid.

Credit cards. When buying goods or tickets and paying hotel or phone bills, you will be asked: "Cash or charge?", meaning you have the choice of paying in cash or by credit card. Businesses are wary of little-known credit cards, but they'll gladly accept major American or international cards.

Many service stations and other businesses will not take money at night, only cards. Outside normal office hours, it's sometimes impossible to hire cars and pay bills with cash.

You'll need to show some form of identification when charging your purchase.

Traveller's cheques. Visitors from abroad may find traveller's cheques drawn on American banks easier to cash than those on foreign banks. Cash small amounts at a time, keeping the balance of your cheques in the hotel safe if possible. It's a good idea to follow instructions given for recording where and when you cashed each cheque.

Prices. In Greater Miami, most prices do not include a state sales tax of 6%. Hotels add a resort/bed tax of 5% (Surfside 2%, Bal Harbour 3%) to the bill.

The U.S. has a larger range of prices for the same item than you will find anywhere else, as well as a greater choice of goods. For moderately priced articles, visit the big department stores. Small independent grocery stores, drugstores and 24-hour "convenience stores" have higher prices, but independent service stations are cheaper than those of the large oil companies.

NEWSPAPERS and MAGAZINES. Two daily papers are published in Greater Miami: the *Miami Herald* and its Spanish-language edition, *El Miami Herald*, widely read throughout the Americas, and *Diario Las Americas*, aimed at a growing Hispanic readership in the United States. The *Miami Beach Sun Reporter* comes out several times a week.

You can purchase local newspapers and the daily *USA Today* from street-corner vending machines and at newsstands (often in drugstores and convenience stores). Larger newsstands and vending machines in certain locations carry the *New York Times, Wall Street Journal* and a selection of other American papers. The London Sunday papers are available several days after publication at a few larger newsstands (refer to the *Yellow Pages* under "News Dealers").

Supermarkets and newsstands all over Miami carry a selection of national and international magazines, as well as the local monthly **121**

N *Miami/South Florida,* and its Spanish-language counterpart *Miami,* featuring a comprehensive calendar of events. Widely available, too, are *South Florida Home and Garden* and *Florida Trend,* a magazine of business and finance.

P **PHOTOGRAPHY**. Camera shops sell film, but drugstores and supermarkets supply the same at discount prices. Do not leave film anywhere in the car: it will be ruined in the heat.

Airport security machines may damage film. Ask for it to be checked separately, or buy a film shield.

POLICE. City police are concerned with local crime and traffic offences. Highway Patrol officers (also called State Troopers) ensure highway safety and are on the lookout for people speeding or driving under the influence of alcohol or drugs.

Don't hesitate to approach any police officer for information or assistance; helping you is part of their job.

The police emergency number is 911.

PUBLIC HOLIDAYS. If a holiday, such as Christmas Day, falls on a Sunday, banks and most stores close the following day. There are also long weekends (e.g. the one following Thanksgiving) when offices are closed for four days. Many restaurants never shut, however, even at Christmas.

New Year's Day	January 1
Martin Luther King Day	Third Monday in January
Washington's Birthday*	Third Monday in February
Memorial Day	Last Monday in May
Independence Day	July 4
Labor Day	First Monday in September
Columbus Day*	Second Monday in October
Veterans' Day	November 11
Thanksgiving Day	Fourth Thursday in November
Christmas Day	December 25

*Shops and businesses open

R **RADIO and TV**. Miami has several dozen AM and FM radio stations, broadcasting everything from country, Latin and rock to rhythm-and-blues. Some stations feature religious programmes, others are dedicated to talk, and there are those that broadcast in Spanish only. There's one classical music radio station, WTMI, 93.1 F.M. on the dial.

Television is on the air from 6 a.m. to 3 a.m. Local news and sports programmes can be seen at 6 p.m., followed by national and international news at 6.30 or 7, and again at 11 p.m. The shows produced by the major American networks are the staple of Miami television, though local offerings in Spanish and English provide a certain regional flavour. There are no commercials on the educational Public Broadcasting Service (channel 2), which produces its own excellent news and information programmes, in addition to music, dance and natural science features. Cable television, available in many hotels and motels, gives access to several dozen channels.

For a list of weekly television programmes, consult *TV Guide*—sold at newsstands everywhere—or the TV magazines published by the *Miami Herald* (Sunday), which also carries radio information.

RELIGIOUS SERVICES. Saturday newspapers publish information about religious services in the Greater Miami area. In addition to Protestant, Roman Catholic and Greek Orthodox churches, Miami has numerous synagogues and other places of worship. Non-denominational services are held in Everglades National Park on Sundays at 9 a.m. (Flamingo Campground Amphitheater) and 5 p.m. (Long Pine Key Campground Amphitheater).

TIME and DATES. The continental United States has a total of four time zones; Florida (like New York) is on Eastern Standard Time. In summer (between April and October) Daylight Saving Time is adopted and clocks move ahead an hour.

The following chart shows the time in various cities in winter when it's noon in Miami:

Los Angeles	**Miami**	London	Sydney
9 a.m.	**noon**	5 p.m.	4 a.m.
Sunday	**Sunday**	Sunday	Monday

For the exact time, call 324-8811.

Dates in the U.S. are written in a different form from that of Britain; for example, 1/6/99 means January 6, 1999.

T **TIPPING.** Waiters and waitresses earn most of their wages from tips; often they are paid little else. Restaurants do not normally add a service charge. Cinema and theatre ushers and petrol station attendants do not expect anything extra. Some further suggestions:

Porter, per bag	50¢-$1 (minimum $1)
Hotel maid, per week	$3-5
Waiter	15%
Lavatory attendant	25¢
Taxi driver	15%
Guide	10-15%
Hairdresser/Barber	15%

TOILETS. You will find toilets in most public buildings, including department stores, theatres and petrol stations. Public beaches and large recreational parks usually provide toilet facilities. In some places you have to pay; in others you should leave a tip for the attendant.

Americans use the terms "rest room", "powder room", "bathroom" (private) and "ladies" or "men's room" to indicate the toilet.

TOURIST INFORMATION AGENCIES. There can be few places in the world with as much tourist literature as Greater Miami. You are strongly urged to write ahead of time for brochures, specifying your particular area of interest (accommodation, attractions, events, sports).

United States Travel Service
22 Sackville Street
London W1X 2EA (tel. 01-439 7433)

or:

Florida Division of Tourism in Europe
18-24 Westbourne Grove
London W2 5RH (tel. 01-727 1661)

or:

Greater Miami Convention & Visitors Bureau
701 Brickell Avenue, Suite 2700
Miami, FL 33131 (tel. 539-3000 or 1-800-283-2707)

TRANSPORT (see also under Aɪʀᴘᴏʀᴛꜱ and Cᴀʀ ʜɪʀᴇ). Miami is not a town for walking: you'll require some form of transport to make your way around the 27 municipalities of the greater metropolitan area. For most tourists, a car offers the greatest mobility, but there are alternatives.

Metrorail. Miami's futuristic rapid transit system speeds passengers through the city on a 21-mile elevated guideway that runs north-to-south—from Hialeah to South Dade via Government Center, downtown. Trains run daily at 7½-minute intervals in rush hours, 15 minutes at other times. They operate from 6 a.m. to midnight.

Have the exact fare ready in coins (no pennies or half-dollars accepted). For a small additional charge, passengers may transfer from Metrorail to Metrobus. Transfers to Metromover are free.

Metromover. This fully automated "people mover" system provides rapid transit within the downtown area. Metrorail passengers can transfer to Metromover at Government Center station.

Metrobus. Designed to feed into the Metrorail system, Metrobus provides outlying areas with express, local and shuttle service. Bus stops are indicated by the word "Metrobus" and the distinctive blue and green logo of the Metro-Dade Transportation System. The driver will stop only on request. There is only one terminal, in the city of Coral Gables. Seats in the front of the bus are reserved for the elderly and handicapped. Pay the exact fare in coins to the driver when you board. Don't forget to ask for a transfer if you intend to connect to Metrorail.

Taxis. Depending on the company they belong to, vehicles may be painted one of several different colours. However, they always carry a lighted sign. The rates—high throughout the greater metropolitan area—are generally painted on the doors. Apart from the airport taxi rank, it's rare to find cabs waiting for passengers. You'll have to telephone one of the various companies, listed in the *Yellow Pages* under "Taxicabs".

WEIGHTS and MEASURES. The United States is one of the few countries still calculating in feet and inches. Americans are gradually becoming familiar with the metric system, but as yet there is no official changeover programme.

Milk and fruit juice are sold by the quart, or half gallon, although wine and spirits now come in litre bottles. Food products usually have the weight marked in ounces and pounds, as well as in grammes.

W **WINE and SPIRITS**. Supermarkets sell beer and wine, while licenced liquor or "package" stores (off-licenced) sell spirits. Each municipality has its own laws governing the sale and consumption of alcohol. In general, liquor stores are allowed to open for business from 9 a.m. to 8 p.m. Monday to Saturday, and supermarkets are prohibited from selling beer or wine on Sundays before 1 p.m. Beer is available for sale in some parks in Greater Miami, and the consumption of alcohol is allowed on beaches and in larger recreational parks in most municipalities.

Never drink and drive. The Florida Highway Patrol routinely uses breathalysers, and driving while drunk is viewed increasingly as a serious offence.

You must be over 21 to purchase beer or any other alcoholic drink, or to buy any alcohol at a liquor store. You will be asked for identification (called "I.D.") of your age.

Index

An asterisk (*) next to a page number indicates a map reference. For index to Practical Information, see inside front cover.